PRAISE F(

"What I love about this book is that it is both entertaining and insightful. Lynn's stories made me laugh out loud and also gave me an opportunity to consider ways I could find more joy in even the hard or unexpected moments in my life. Whether you're in the throes of toddler tantrums, teenagers, or motherhood surprises of your own, this delightful read and will surely make you smile!"

—Michelle McCollough, speaker, strategist, success coach, serial entrepreneur, show host, author of *The Marketing Blueprint*

"Lynn's honesty and wisdom are a gift to parents. I recommend this book to all moms and dads who've ever been stuck or who are seeking to expand with new perspectives."

—Kyle Wilson, marketer, speaker, founder of Jim Rohn International and KyleWilson.com

"Reading Lynn's words will make you laugh, cry, and recognize that we're all in the same boat, whether you're a brand new mom or you've been around the block a time or two. In short, I found myself reflected in her story. This is not a 'let-me-tell-you-how-it's-done' kind of book. *The Perfect Cupcake* is mom-ing, sisterhood, and solidarity in a delightful, easy-to-read, and hilarious memoir about a pivot in priorities following a completely unexpected 'curveball.' It's absolutely a must read and must share for moms of any age, phase, or situation!"

—Leslie Judd, extraordinary mom, entrepreneur and life-long learner

"Very funny and open-hearted, this fresh perspective on motherhood is a read that every woman can enjoy."

—Takara Sights, author, editor, writing coach

"Lynn Bodnar's candid, vulnerable look at her experience of unexpected motherhood later in life is a journey through the pain of judgment into the possibility of awareness and choice. The expectations society has around motherhood. The narrow definition of what is allowable and the censure that anything outside that definition 'rightly' receives. The comparisons and expectations we hold up as 'this is how a good mother does things' many times without ever asking 'says who!' Ms. Bodnar's humor and willingness to shine a light on what else we might choose is a breath of fresh air in an arena that can feel stifling. For me this work is an invitation to kindness: kindness to ourselves and others. Kindness in thought, word, and deed that can open a whole new world of possibilities."

—Julie Margo, Full Spectrum Self, Access Bars Facilitator

"*The Perfect Cupcake* tells the genuine story of motherhood and the wide range of emotions that role encompasses in a heartfelt yet often humorous way. *The Perfect Cupcake* is a truly delightful read. Lynn has chosen to be 'real' to her readers, and by doing so, encourages all of us to be real with each other."

—Jessica Mullen, intentional mom, entrepreneur

"*The Perfect Cupcake* takes us on a humorous yet thoughtful romp through the many impossible expectations that swirl through a mom's head. And, speaking of impossible, a one in 17 million occurrence helps author Lynn Bodnar burst through all those expectations to bring readers nine realizations about what really matters—as parents and as humankind."

—Diane Ingram Fromme, mom, stepmom, and author of *Stepparenting the Grieving Child*

"Lynn Bodnar (mama of 4) offers her story of embracing unexpected change, rejecting outdated societal norms, and finding a new level of self-trust and acceptance with grace, vulnerability, and humor. Beautifully combining relatability, hilarious stories, and anecdotal lessons, *The Perfect Cupcake* will validate and uplift moms to a new level of 'I've GOT this.'"

—Sarah Zeren, hybrid coach and counselor, Through the Looking Glass

"Lynn's open and vulnerable look at awareness of self is refreshing and an important reminder of what all moms need to do to survive the harsh judgment we feel from others AND ourselves. Besides motherhood being one of the most important 'careers' on the planet, it's also one of the most underrated and difficult roles a woman will experience in her lifetime. Thank you, Lynn, for talking about the 'non-discussables' that every mom thinks about, but very few openly talk about!"

—Donna Cuddemi, phenom mom, voiceover artist

"Lynn Bodnar shows us how to get through the muck and mire of a life event with wit, humor, and great insight. Each page will have you nodding your head in agreement. Great book that speaks to us all."

—Cyndee Jardieu, mother of four, coach and author of *Detour to Happiness*

"Her writing style is just like her in person. It's her conversation and familiarity and humor by opening herself up and presenting truth—raw, human, heart and soul exposed. It is like sitting down and having a REAL conversation with your best friend (because nobody else is going to expose their heart and soul to that degree). The here-you-go-realness-and-I-hope-my-story-can-help."

—Sue Fitch, mom, entrepreneur, owner of The Cacao Forge

The
Perfect
Cupcake
a m♥moir

Lynn Bodnar

Photography by Dayton Williams and Mark Wiens

Cover and book design by Chelsea Jewell

Name: Bodnar, Lynn, author.

Title: The Perfect Cupcake / Lynn Bodnar.

Description: First trade paperback original edition. | Colorado : Art of Momliness LLC, 2019

Identifiers: ISBN-13: 978-0-9977944-5-8

Subjects: BISAC: BIOGRAPHY & AUTOBIOGRAPHY / Personal Memoirs. | FAMILY & RELATIONSHIPS / Parenting / Motherhood. | HUMOR / Topic / Marriage & Family.

MANUFACTURED IN THE UNITED STATES OF AMERICA

First Edition

To the only four people in the whole wide world who can call me Mom: Brandon, Blake, Brooke, and Brianna. I love and adore you all—you are my joy, purpose, grounding, and perfected cupcakes.

To my husband EJ: look at what two high school sweethearts have built! I wouldn't trade it for anything, and I wouldn't have built it with anyone else. Thank you for your love, patience, and commitment to me and this family. (And, I think we're done with bonus babies now, right?)

TO CONNECT WITH THE AUTHOR

Lynn Bodnar
the heart of the matter

Check out The Momoir Series on YouTube
Facebook: Heart of the Matter, Lynn Bodnar
Join the private group, Heart of the Matter, Village
Website: lynnbodnar.com

TABLE OF CONTENTS

INTRODUCTION   xi

1   How it all Started   01

2   Be a Good Mom, Sit…Stay   11

3   Judgment Daze   21

4   Wait… What?   33

5   Telling Others was Really Telling   59

6   What Once Seemed so Important…   81

7   The Final ~~Denial~~ Countdown   99

8   The Big Day   117

9   Delivering a New Me   135

ABOUT THE AUTHOR   177

GRATITUDES   179

🌿 INTRODUCTION 🌿

Once upon a time, there was a maiden. She lived an average life within an average story. Charmed by Prince Charming himself, she married, had children (that's when she got her full name, Mom! Mom! Mom!), and pursued motherhood awesomeness in her fairytale castle. She had worked hard, built a career and then a family—a life. She cruised around in her mini-carriage, and her life quickly became the familiar:

- eat
- get kids to sports
- worry about stuff
- sleep
- repeat

Amazingly blessed, grateful, livin' the dream: she was focused on the job at hand, growing her children. Life was "perfect" and wonderful by all accounts. That's how it goes, right?

Slowly, her life seemed to revert to the pre-princess Cinderella times (on call with a mop, ready with the perfect classroom snack, and all that "they" say it takes to be a "good mom"). She began to wonder and sing randomly with cartoon birds. Occasionally, she even talked with mice.

But…

I'm average, she thought. *I've felt average for quite a while. That's okay, right?*

The mice agreed. "So, you gonna be okay with that, Momerelli?" asked the mice.

Average in this culture is just not gonna be enough—it has rockstar requirements or you just get stuck with the mice. No offense, guys.

But it got worse. I (um, I mean, the princess) listened to the stories of my "just a mom" inadequate average-ness.

They were delivered in subtle ways, like (picture a random mom at school, put together, clean hair, pointing a manicured index finger)…

"Staying home and baking the cookies for every event is great, but really, how long does that take, and who can't do that?"

But, wait, that's not all I do… I…

"Your child will really be less developed and adaptable without daycare because you don't have the ability to provide ALL that well-researched and well-rounded, fully staffed daycare experience."

Wow, my kid could really be behind. I know it wasn't my major, but I come up with some good stuff. We are working on phonics 'cause he just turned six months old… that counts, right?

"OH MY GOSH!! I would go stir-crazy staying home. I'd be bored to tears within a week. What do you actually do, I mean to even stay sane? You are sane, right?"

Sometimes, sane, yes. On the weeks I get to sleep. As far as what I do well, it varies by day, how much time do you have for me to tell you about it, and by the way, what day is it?

"I mean, COME ON, Lynn. Without a paycheck and paying taxes, do you really think you are a contribution to society or a drain?"

Well, my husband and I have a partnership. Not sure he could actually afford to outsource all my labor. Does it really all tie into transactional dollars?

"You had a fun career, traveling all the time. How do you just stop and not use your brain and education anymore?"

I kind of remember that person. Maybe she could tutor my kid. I must have her over for some wine. If I remember, she likes red.

"Of course, everyone would LOVE to be on permanent vacay and be provided for, but not everyone is lucky like you."

Actually, vacays are even more work, so… wait, what?

"You have it so easy—no job, no boss, no office, no hours. You can wear whatever you want, eat whenever, and go wherever. I can't imagine you have a complaint in the world!"

Why do I even try to answer, feel defensive about my choices, as if I owe an explanation? Why is it fair game to make any and all thoughtless comments to moms? Even worse, deep down, oh my gosh, could they be right?

These insidious thoughts created a story of inadequacy that would continue in my head. "Bah, Lynn, look at these people at this party. Your life is SO predictable that they won't even talk to you. They don't ask about your day or interests or 'how's the job going?' because they think they already know. Their assumptions are their answers. Or worse, they risk your response being more boring than they can handle and they may not have a clear exit strategy."

More surprising than these comments, was the realization that even a "safe place" working with fellow moms at school or activities, seemed to develop into a zero-sum game. Perhaps other frustrated and unvalidated moms were just trying to reach for some cred: "Yeah, that's right. I showed that PTA who's boss. Made the principal cry, too." Or, "I dominated the room-mom gig, no question." It could be like, "Wait, you only served ice cream cups at your classroom party? I made ice cream from scratch, to order, in mine. I'll help you next time."

This glimmer of hope to be more than just average (like a B– or even a B) was a direct result of feeling that I was figuring out parenting—at least at home. Intuitively, with study, trial and error, intelligence—I mean, I was all in. When I shared my ideas, several others were like, "Wow, great idea," or "Great approach." One of my friends actually credits me for her being a better parent by implementing my "Lynn-isms." Wow. It's just that none of it came with promotions, feedback, office parties, bonuses, validation, or even proof that I was doing it "right". The mom training program stops when you step out of the hospital door with your counting-on-you-to-figure-this-out-and-keep-me-alive-and-thriving bundle of joy. No pressure.

However, we all know where social respectability stems from: the mighty W2, where the amount on the page dictates your effort and thus proves you have a brain, value and ambitions. In a paying job, year after year, even a small increase in pay proves you are worth something, that you show up and demonstrate your value, and that you're committed. Who would continue to get paid if corporate America didn't see that, right? For the stay-at-home moms, the respectability comes when, in eighteen short years, wait for it... we'll see how she did on the job. And we'll judge the pants off that, especially if one of the kids "goes awry".

On the other hand, if the average mom doesn't show up for the job, even for a few hours, she is rewarded with free room and board. In jail for neglect. Yep, still a freeloader.

With the claws of my inner dialogue digging in and continuing to hijack my confidence, I just carried on as is. I just thought, hey, we were living the average American life, not the exciting kind that is on the news, and that's fine. Just an average family (well, actually above average, with three whole kids instead of the 2.5 American average— rocked that!).

After several years of this existence and just as I began to think about heading back out into the "real" world, I received the shock of my life. The audacity of the universe throwing me a curveball. Against all odds, I found myself pregnant in my forty-third year of life. A whole five-and-a-half years after the snip, you know, the big V (vasectomy). Maybe it was that intrusive, clueless, absentminded, wand-happy fairy godmother? Or that, unbeknownst to us and anyone we've ever known, things grow back. Either way, life as I knew it would stop in its tracks. And I would have to stop with it and face some reality.

How could an unexpected—no, "impossible"—pregnancy at this late stage of the game create or lead me to personal discovery and the expanded awareness that I was asleep, literally on autopilot? I'd been going along, trying to do the mom gig based on everyone else's rules about how to show up and when. "Mandatory" this and "your kids will be behind" that. Scared to death of another pregnancy, especially with the potentially daunting physical damages. Blind to my own numbness and victim-mode thinking; compliant, criticism-phobic, and generally hiding my potential. I was ready to scream—What are we doing? Why do we do it this way? Says who? Why is this happening? Who the heck am I?

In parallel, I was subcutaneously terrified to face my denial about not wanting to start over with a newborn when it felt like I "should" embrace the amazing gift I was getting with unquestioned joy and minute-by-minute gratitude. What else would I need to face?

Why be afraid? I've done this pregnancy bit three times before. No mystery to it at this point for me. What was knocking on my knocked-up door was full awareness that not only was I ignorant to asking the "right" questions for ME, but, heck, I was completely ignoring myself. The question of what I desired—me, Mom, Lynn Bodnar—was never really a consideration of mine and, therefore, wasn't on the radar of others. Requiring myself to analyze my life meant I would need to CHANGE. Activate comfort zone obliteration. So, that's how those unexpected two blue lines became a scary vulnerability makeover. Oh yeah, and a new baby. There just might be some new demands with that, at almost forty-three years old, when it was not common and still pretty rare for that "advanced" age.

Okay, Oprah, Brené, Mel, Glennon, Martha, Shonda, Jen, Elizabeth, Rachel, and all y'all, I'm going for it. Here's the story. For real. As is. Based on events that kicked me in the gut, multiple times.

Disclaimer: This story involves a tremendous amount of TMI (yes, "too much information"). Sex, drugs, rock 'n' roll, and international intrigue. Feelings, thoughts, illusions, and owies. Va-jayjays and vas deferens. If this and more bother you, well, you've been forewarned.

1

How it all Started

We were really fortunate, my husband and I. When we decided that we were ready to start a family, it came easily. I remember telling my husband to be patient, we could expect it to take about six months to get pregnant because I traveled every week with my job. Turned out not to be the case. One and done. It was strangely unexpected because everybody talked a lot about "trying". Are you trying? How's it going? You guys trying? Takes a while when you're trying, y'know. Even with our intentions to make a baby and start the "trying", somehow, it was still a surprise when it happened. Like, wow, this is the real deal now. No turning back. Bun is officially in oven. The EPT said so.

Becoming a first-time parent brought so many changes, surprises, new experiences, and learnings. I learned how much I didn't know, and how much I thought I knew just from observation or from babysitting fifteen years before—hilarious. This first baby paved the way, as the oldest often does in many things, including physically creating permanent changes in my body, and, y'know, my stuff. Natural childbirth, although honestly preferred by me and required to sound tough among my peers, equals natural destruction of some girl parts. Don't freak—all livable and kind of restored after some recovery time. Like ten years.

Many moms say to their kids, "You have NO IDEA what I went through to have you!" Probably a good thing kids don't remember their birth. But moms do. There is no way to forget. Deep down, we may just want the respect from our kids, like, "Holy crap, you did what? I will never, ever talk back, fail to load the dishwasher, or question you ever again, you power goddess you." Even with my first birthing experience, which included eighteen hours of labor, sixteen inches of snowfall that resulted in an absent doctor and the instructions to stop pushing at 2 a.m. (which is like telling someone mid-vomit to hold back—impossible), and an "above average" amount of stitches and bleeding, I got the job done. I felt, strangely, somewhat in control in an out-of-control situation. It was an interesting intro to childbirth.

The next two "tries" ended in miscarriage. That was a confusing and difficult time for me. The notions of "oh, just try again", "sometimes things are not meant to be", and "maybe something was wrong both times and it's for the better" were hard for me to just accept. I went down a path of wondering what I had done wrong. I wondered if it would even be possible to have more children. So, I just did what everyone said, I would just carry on, despite the fear of it happening again, and do as suggested—try again. My German doctor bluntly said to me, right after miscarrying three months into a pregnancy, "Go home. Wait a month, and then do it."

My second angel weighed in at 10 lbs., 4 oz. Okay, now freak out. But, yes… I did walk again. Last week. I'd said from the start that boy was born hunky and happy. But there were some, let's say, challenges. He was born in Germany, and they seemed to be clueless as to his robust makeup. The fact that I was a walking house wasn't enough of a clue, I guess.

As the labor proceeded in the drugless fashion that I'd lost my mind to choose, I have to say, I was in the zone: working with my body, knowing what to expect with round two, focused, all systems go. Everyone was speaking English, giving me routine encouragement, the woman on the bed trying to make this deal happen. His head emerged (embrace the TMI), and the umbilical cord was wrapped around his neck. Everyone suddenly switched to urgently speaking German, but somehow, I understood most of what they were saying (I could speak some of this long-worded language by living there). It was a panic situation.

The room was hot and getting hotter with the smell of everyone's sweat joining with mine. I clearly remember praying, *God help me* and getting the answer, "Better go all out or this is not gonna end well for one or both of us." I went for it, and after a bit, miraculously, his stuck shoulders emerged as did the rest of him. Didn't want to even think of the new anatomy I had "down there"… I mean, this was a Geronimo-yelling, whiskey-downin', bullet-biting, no-holds-barred effort. But good thing because they were alternating between (I found out later) breaking my pelvis or his shoulders. The Herr Doktor told me we were very lucky he didn't have a "gimp" arm—it's literally what he said. Either way, it sent shivers down my spine. Didn't remember reading about this deal in any "delivering your baby" books or *What to Expect When You Are Expecting*.

Funny thing, they had to rush him off to the Kinderclinic (NICU), and the midwife (which is an automatic requirement in Germany— stayed with me and the Herr Doktor the whole time) said, "Okay, *she* is fine, we must review her." And with that the teams exited with my hard-earned baby. I looked at my husband and said, "She? I saw a stem on that apple!" His face was sheet-white after the ordeal. He said, "Wrong pronoun—HE is our baby boy." Thankfully, all was well; my boy was fine, and I would live to tell the tale (and wear pants again). My husband would recover too. Can't imagine what that was like from his perspective. I barely felt that I was even in my own body. More floating somewhere in the vicinity.

Life in Germany with my three-and-a-half-year-old boy and a newborn was pretty charmed. Deliciously simple. We would walk or bike to the market almost every day due to our small refrigerator and get that day's food. There was always an open-air market with all the basics and more: different carts for meats, cheeses, fish, breads, veggies and fruits, milk, and of course, pastries and desserts and Bretzeln for the kids (yeah, with a B, that's how you say it there, I fought that for a while too). On Tuesdays, they had roasted chickens—score! The sights, smells and sounds were always so fresh as people just went about their business. It allowed me a certain ease into this role of mother of two, a peaceful and fairly confident transition. Not easy, just different demands. I learned simple things like coordinating how to bike to the market with two kids and where to put the food (in the bike basket, but sometimes I had a backpack too). I enjoyed just attending to the basics and focusing on the daily needs of my two children and the home. My plan was coming together perfectly. Little did I know I would look back on this relatively calm time so fondly.

I came across a Krabbel gruppe (play group) for small children at the local school that summer, and we would go there so my then three-and-a-half-year-old could get all his energy out. Okay, like ten percent. It was pretty cool how there were all sorts of nationalities there. But German was spoken, so I had to do my best to understand and respond in un-weird, non-awkward ways. Truthfully, in hindsight, it was actually nice to be fairly clueless. God bless language barriers—or at least not understanding everything. I didn't completely know if I was being judged, ridiculed, considered not good enough, totally good enough, embraced, or just tolerated. Ah, the ignorant bliss of it all.

When that newborn baby boy suddenly turned into a one-year-old (with the adorable attempts at speech filling the air), my husband and I were sitting over dinner and had the "are we done?" conversation. I looked at our family picture and said that I really saw another face in the frame. My mate agreed, so I had my way with him.

A little while later, I went into the German doctor's office to verify this third pregnancy (with the miscarriage fears still nagging just under the surface). While in the waiting room another American woman approached me. She said she'd heard me speaking German and was wondering if I could help her. *Of course*, I thought, *we are in this often confusing and foreign situation together*. She took me aside and tearfully told me her story of being pregnant, completely freaked out, kind-of not wanting to have another child (would be her fourth), and her husband was totally NOT okay with it. She needed to speak to the doctor about having an abortion, but she didn't speak any German, and she wanted to make sure the conversation was going to be clear. Could I help translate? She was shaking, afraid, hurting, alone and it broke my heart.

Feeling really awkward concerning such a deeply personal situation, I told her I thought the doctor would be fine discussing this with her in English. I wasn't even sure I was the right person for translating the words for her, honestly, not that great at German. The doctors also spoke English very well. She seemed uncertain, bewildered, and scared about everything and, really, I think just wanted someone with her. She was emotionally raw and wrecked. I just wanted to support her, give her the love she needed. I could actually feel how alone she felt. She was clearly torn up as a mom and a woman. I'll never know what happened, what she ended up choosing. It was such a contrast: that day of my bliss and her anguish.

So, my third child was manufactured in Germany and born in Colorado. Yep, doing my part to bring jobs to America. We made this huge international move to a rental home when I was in my first trimester and then moved again into a home we built within three weeks of my due date. It's so awesome to reduce stress like that. My husband was adjusting to his new job in the States and covering stuff in Germany—working all sorts of hours. I'm not sure he really knew I was expecting.

Everything just seemed blurred together, but I knew it would be okay. It was all part of the plan: Get the shipment from Germany and inspect all that for damage. Get our (dusty) boxes of stuff that had been in storage for almost four years, and inspect all of that, also within sixty days. Make the damage claims and follow up. Take care of toddlers. Repack things for the move to our permanent house. Try to not puke from morning sickness. Adjust back to America, friendless, but there was ice in our drinks and stores open twenty-four hours. Yep, it was all coming together.

The OB/GYN doc back here in America watched me like a hawk because of the size of my previous son. We hadn't actually known the birthweight for baby number two because they gave it to us in grams. At the time, I was so exhausted and my husband wasn't focused on it, so we never did the math to be exact. I mentioned the birthweight to the doctor, and for some reason, said it in grams, "Like 4700 grams or something." He was like, "Wait a sec. Then whipped out his calculator, and said, "Oh boy—that was ten pounds, four ounces!!" *Wa, wa ... what?* That was news to me. At this point, I was almost three months pregnant and started hurting (and sweating) all over again and requested a wheelchair. He started ordering gestational diabetes tests on the hour. Kidding—every other hour.

My labor was induced with baby number three to avoid overtime, so to speak. No extra innings, thank you. The doctor and my husband talked me into an epidural. I say that 'cause they did, but I blame myself for not saying no. It was not something I wanted at all. It's crazy, of course, and I certainly do not judge anyone else's preference. But for me, I liked working with my body, having control, and certainly being able to stand up when the delivery was done, so I could move around and take a shower. It wasn't some macho thing, just a personal preference. Did I mention having control?

I felt disoriented and confused; it was hard to work with my body on the juice. I was distracted by the strange metallic taste in my mouth. I couldn't really tell when a productive contraction was going on unless the doc said something, or I could see the little blue wavy lines on the monitor. So, I felt I couldn't maximize the effort and had to guess. I didn't know how hard I was pushing or how effectively. Gosh, I really was a labor nerd. Besides the lack of control in the whole effort, and this may surprise you, I very much disliked not being in control of my legs. I was promised it was only short term. Just during the major throes of the labor process. Or so they said…

My paranoia played out. Even though they promised to turn off the juice the second they could, apparently there was a "shift change" and it was left on. My lower half was left entirely asleep. I was paralyzed and pissed off for three-and-a-half more hours. My husband felt badly, and I was going with the flow because I decided to be a good sport. Or didn't have an option. All a result of my not speaking up for myself.

Of course, when she was born, and they held her up, the joy of her sweet, healthy entrance into this world was really all I needed. SHE was breathtaking. The rest would pass. Not having found out the gender of any of our kids beforehand, it was fun to have the doctor hold her up and say (in English), "She is beautiful and perfect." No confused pronouns. We had a girl. The boys had a sister. Our family was blessed and complete.

I had no idea what changes might be waiting downstairs with this one—all part of the story—because I couldn't feel anything at that moment. Did I mention the overtime use of epidural? Not bitter…

The Snip

After the dust settled (read "stitches dissolved"), my proactive dutiful husband, as per the completed family picture agreement, scheduled his vasectomy, without hesitation. We had our three delicious munchkins, and we had agreed we were done. I know some women have had to put together an entire PowerPoint presentation on why their husbands need to get the snip. He just needed to see me go through labor three times to know that a little snip and a twenty-four-hour date with a bag of frozen peas was nothing to fuss about. Well, he did a little fussing. He is a Y chromosome person after all—they do that. Very little though.

By the way, I was there. I witnessed it. The whole procedure. More out of interest, like watching the Discovery Channel. And it was fascinating. In the bright and sterile smelling outpatient procedure room, the doctor obliged me by explaining things as he went. I found it really interesting. The doc was really into it, enjoying the audience and providing a tutorial. He was carrying on and saying, "You do this and want to be sure to cauterize here AND here." Then he slipped out another noodley-vein-looking thing and said, "Some people get in trouble forgetting to take care of this little guy too."

I was like, get in trouble?

But at that moment he also said, "EJ, are you doing okay up there?"

EJ lifted his head up and said, "Yeah, fine."

All of a sudden it hit me that all those parts and interesting bits were EJ's stuff. The room, for some reason, started to spin (it spun faster, and faster, and then everything was still, absolutely still). I connected the interesting guts to actually being my husband's stuff. I had to sit down, and the doctor told a nurse to check on me and make sure I hadn't fainted. Guess I wasn't tough enough to be looking at these insides after all. Somehow, it's super cool until it's connected to a loved one. Then it's raw and real and somewhat intense. So, I was mostly there and witnessed everything. The big snip had happened.

With the almost fainting incident, we paid no attention

to the little "get into trouble" bit. He went home and sat on his bag of frozen peas, and it was done. Funny how kids can wonder, "Are we still going to eat those peas?" He also returned as required, like a good soldier, for all the proper post-procedure checkups. No swimmers. We were officially done. Finito. No mas. As per the plan.

I was in the charmed-life zone. Knowing I was done having babies, I could now focus on the different stages my three kids were at. Each day brought me so many cool things to see through their eyes, so much laughter, exploration, and new "wows" to enjoy. Butterflies, dirt, fireworks, animals, and holding hands with new little friends seemed beyond amazing to each of them. From making forts out of boxes and chasing rainbows and frogs, to looking for fairies in the woods. From marveling at their sandcastle masterpieces to tears as the waves moved in closer and swept it all away. My front seat view of watching their thought processes was astonishing and hilarious. They were demanding, but it was all what I had hoped for, and I was present and grateful and loved the family picture with its growing little faces each year. I was thankful we had made this plan—all our hopes and dreams for a family—come true. I was enjoying this promotion to mother of three and felt each kid brought me a new level of ability—a feeling of, "I've got this".

Be a Good Mom, Sit... Stay

So, there we had it: three beautiful children, one dog, two fish, and a snip. Life was how it was supposed to be. I was ready to mom it up, figure it out. Dominate, er, uh, mominate! Focus on this mom-a-thon for the next eighteen plus-years and beyond, always being awesome and "on it".

Like all moms and dads, I just jumped in and started to learn how to raise kids, how to do this undefined job in this modern society. I made the huge choice to be a stay-at-home mom, so I was going to figure this out and be the best mom ever! (Echo: ever! ever! ever!) I would earn the mug. Give fuel to future Mother's Day cards. Create the wise "My mom always said..." sayings.

All In

I was idealistic, and I was all in. I really wanted to be a great mom to these three (while also promising myself not to lose

myself in the process). To me, that included providing for
them, being a source of comfort, strength, and safety; being
their foundation; being abundantly available; and providing
a loving "kick in the pants" when needed. I would teach and
model life lessons on everything and on how to navigate this
world. I would be the person they'd trust to tell them the
truth of what a word really meant. Like when my son heard
the word "bee-an" in second grade. What? Oh, you heard
the word *lesbian*. Okay, let's chat, I will tell you the truth as
I've always promised and I will answer all your questions the
best I can. I always believed it was better to hear it from me
than from an ignorant, confused, or uneducated peer.

I believed there was a fine balance between when not to
be there (ground that helicopter) and knowing when it was
time to cry with them, to feel the pain, and make sense of
friends being mean (and to check their mean-o-meter too).

I would marvel at all the moments. So many moments: the
brave, chin-quivering goodbye at preschool and kindergarten,
getting on the bus for the first time, feeling the connection to
their own power by training the puppy, eye-rolling awkward
laughing in the third grade musical, heartfelt tears reading
Where the Red Fern Grows, playing hide-and-go-seek with my
go-to, they-will-never-find-me spot which to this day is in
the cleaning supplies closet. Weird they don't know where
that is…

I was living the saying, "The days are long and the
years are short" but didn't really know it at the time. I was
holding on to the idyllic times that had started my mom
journey, including the experience in Germany, enjoying
those moments of pure wonder and discovery on my
children's faces. I was grateful to see first steps and hear first
words. Those delicious times they fell asleep on me I will

never forget. Their first laughs are a treasure in my heart, and when they can wrap their little arms around your neck for a real "I mean it" hug, what in the whole world is better than that?

You're Doing It Wrong...

Outside of my little world, though, subtle little clues began to hint that I should be doing things differently, that I should pay better attention to the obvious and not so obvious. Soon I was seeing them everywhere. For example, in preschool, it's pretty common for the kids to create an "All About Me" poster and experience their first presentation. Cool stuff. Without much guidance from the teacher, I helped my child choose some of her favorite things, peppered with some family info: books, treats, movies, siblings, pets. I guided her with her project, she put together the masterpiece, and we showed up on the day they were due.

My jaw dropped as I saw the other kids' poster-board presentations. Pixar would've been jealous. These kids were amazing three- and four-year-olds! Looking at "our" poster, with the half-eaten gummy candy hanging off (I mean, after all, it's her favorite treat and there is an entire car ride to school), stickers randomly scattered in a way that made sense to my child, and with some dog hair sticking to it, I quickly learned I missed the message. *I* was supposed to make it look amazing, not my kid. She would have her turn to make her own "All About Me" poster another day. When she was a parent.

A few moms were so complimentary. "Is that your daughter's poster?! Well, isn't that ... cute." I got the distinct feeling they may not have meant that sincerely.

Other things, cultural things, expectations of the role of mom, also slowly crept in, like, "Mom, you had better get it right." You need to do it all. When listening to or talking with other parents, it seemed like there was no room for mistakes. Who knew what screwing up looked like? Really won't know 'til the late teen years, right? Arriving back to the States from Germany after living there for almost four years, I was out of touch on what was most relevant, the latest "should's". There suddenly was so much I didn't know, and lives were at stake here. The entire futures of my children would hang on my proper research and impeccable decision-making.

When my oldest was heading into kindergarten, I experienced relentless questioning as to where he would go to elementary school. Are you doing bilingual? Core knowledge curriculum? Individualized academics? Home school? Private? Public? IB? Charter? Montessori? Haven't you been researching this for years and already applied to the best schools? If not, you are screwed and you entirely messed up your kid's future.

This was like another foreign language for me to figure out. Completely confused, I would muster an answer of, "I guess the local school assigned to our neighborhood that seems to have good ratings?" I could see the knowing glances, indicating they thought my kid was clearly headed for meth use because his mom was clueless. Maybe I should just cut to the chase and research rehab facilities instead? Is there a 529 for that? I'm sure I would have been too behind in making contributions even if it were a "thing". It was a silent accusation of all that I apparently didn't know.

The pressure around food in general, and "getting that right," was incredible. What are you feeding your kids? Are you nailing the big five every day (veggies, including something green, of course)? You don't actually go to fast food, do you? Everyone acts like they don't and just hopes not to get recognized at the McDonald's drive-thru. I found it pretty funny that no one "ate that junk," but no one questioned the school fund-raisers at the fast food restaurants either. Sadly, though, I have actually corrupted an innocent, perfectly healthy-eating child. Her mother braved letting her come with us after preschool for a playdate. I decided to take the girls to the PlayPlace at McDonald's. I texted the mom and asked her what her daughter usually got at McD's. She replied that she didn't know—it was her first time there. Just like that, my "Mom of the Year" award flew right out the window. Oops.

Why was I missing all this stuff? What was my problem? Could I really mess this up? Should I just plan on their future therapy? What else could thwart my intended awesome mom-a-thon?

My Kryptonite

I thought my main challenge at the time was to figure out the balancing act of having three children. It was a new level of different needs with new idiosyncrasies. And, now I was clearly outmanned—only two hands when three would be needed. A zone defense was not even possible. However, what really started to put me in a hole was the bone-weary, out-of-body lack of sleep. My total kryptonite. I wondered how my mother-in-law did it. She brought eleven children into the world. And raised them. Herself. And remained sane. How was that possible? Heck, if she could rock it with eleven, I should be fine with three. Nothing to complain about. Don't be a wuss.

However, with the chronic lack of sleep and hormone chaos, I quickly became discombobulated, so disconnected from each day and from myself. I was completely fuzzy-headed. When I was awake for the day, it didn't really register that I was awake. It was like walking in a dream state trying to figure out if I was dreaming or not. If I stopped for a second, I would do the chicken head-jerk to not fall asleep where I stood (okay, or at the stoplight in my car; don't tell).

I was pretty on edge… how did I just get in my driveway? Wasn't I just *Starbucks-gazing*? You know, driving by Starbucks, gazing longingly at the entrance, and daydreaming about what it would be like to saunter in with just my wallet. I'd order my Skinny London Fog with coconut milk. I'd actually have showered and put on big-girl clothes. I'd have a brief, real adult conversation in the too-short line, and then I'd enjoy a good book while soaking in the freshly brewed aromas and sipping my drink. Mercifully, Starbucks now has more and more drive-thrus. Moms of small children desperately thank you.

That level of ongoing sleep deprivation has an insidious effect on a person. I tried to just mind-over-matter the condition, but month after month after month of sleeplessness put me and my brain on survival autopilot.

The few and far between mindful moments came like brief rays of sunlight peeking through massive clouds. I was not creating my days, or an intentional plan, and certainly not a goal-oriented future. I was simply reacting to each moment, each issue, day by day. I was trying to connect thoughts together, but it was frustratingly beyond my reach. I found myself regularly asking, "What the heck is happening to my brain?" And then wondering who I was talking to.

My default slowly became infused with what society's messages are about my role and expectations as a mother.

How were the Disney moms handling these issues? What does Dora the Explorer's mom do when Dora goes all freaky tantrum at Target, and her cart is full of frozen stuff and a desperately needed pack of diapers (while everyone is standing around staring and shaking their heads at this terrible mother)? I was living a life of the oxymoronic: physical/brain-fogged sleeplessness AND sleeping my way through life beyond what was in front of me at any given moment. I lived by what I "should" have been doing for my kids according to what "they" said. Planning ahead meant having a full diaper bag with replenished supplies. "New experiences" meant wondering how my hair would look brushed. Tomorrow, I'll...

Sometimes the seductive siren call captured me, leading me to think that maybe tonight I'd get a little sleep. Alas, the tormenting but heart-tugging (and milk-flooding) baby cries throughout the night usually started just as my head would finally hit the pillow. Feed baby, get baby down. Back to my bed, then, what? A toddler nightmare, complete with dragon slayer and monster eradicator duties? What option was there? I had to grab my sword and take care of business. Besides, not responding, the experts said, would cause a lack of trust, broken bonds, and basically produce a serial killer. Again, no pressure there.

The most hilarious (in a way that makes me want to punch someone) advice was "sleep when the baby sleeps". Impossible. Almost cruel. There is a cosmic radar that tunes into that exact moment. Your sweet muffin often falls asleep just a bit too early in the car seat and never transfers to a full nap when you get home ten minutes later. Even if you do get the baby down, remember those other kids? Their needs are ongoing and especially heightened when the baby sleeps. So, you become a crazed woman trying to occupy them (properly as society dictates, no screens, and they should be reading by two years old, advanced algebra not 'til four). If you do get them set up with some brain-advancing activity, how can you think about sleeping when you could be cleaning your house to keep it magazine perfect? Ha! If you do accidentally nod off in the middle of making a PB&J, the doorbell will invariably ring for sure.

Any way I sliced it, I began to realize we moms tend to have a busy, isolated, tiring, and often unvalidated existence. True story: When we had just moved into our rental house after we repatriated, I was pregnant with my third. My oldest was five years old, and my second son was one-and-a-half years old. I was sick as a dog with morning sickness. Every time I stood up, I made a forceful contribution to that porcelain structure, provided I got there in time. But I had the two small kids to take care of, no mom, sister, or even friend to call. My husband was literally working all hours to help folks transition in Germany and ramp up back in America.

I remember my younger son asking over and over for "apple duce." I called on my de-horking powers, grabbed his sippy cup, and crawled to the refrigerator. I did my best to pour as much as possible in the cup so it would last as long as possible. *When did apple juice start smelling so vile?* I crawled it over to him and then crawled back over to the couch. Success! Didn't lose the contents of my stomach. Only to look over at my boys to see them laughing hysterically, thinking I wanted to play a pretend animal game or something. So, I explained the rules of the classic game, Zookeeper. "You be silent animals crawling and hiding, and I'll be the zookeeper on the couch. If I see you, you're out. And hand Mommy that special zookeeper's bucket, sweetie." #artofmomliness

Days like that made to-do lists feel like harsh judges. Sometimes it was the little things that became important or made me feel less frustrated or stuck over never getting through a single to-do list. I always felt I had at least fifty thousand things to check off. What was with the satisfaction of those elusive little checkmarks? Most times, though, I felt like I wasn't "accomplishing" anything for days on end. How could I answer the question, what did I do all day? Some of my "come to terms with it" tactics included things like not allowing my husband to come home from the day and actually ask me, "What did you do today?" It instantly filled me with frustration, guilt, to-do-list incompetence, insecurity, and all-around defensiveness. (But, hey, the kids are good, right?… Where are they anyway?) Not his fault, just how it triggered me. He was instructed to ask me how my day was instead. Fine, thank you, yours? Yes, a simple pleasantry triggered me. (I could blame it on lack of sleep edginess, yeah, that was it.) But then, I also wasn't triggering him by asking about the top five reasons why his marketing program was late to launch, right? How's the marketing budget looking, any overages? "How was your day" worked great for us, with any additional conversation we might be ready to share flowing from there. Or not. Somehow, to-do lists, and other related triggers, were becoming a harsh self-judgment as well.

My body was working through the days and nights to provide for the needs of my children and family. My head was trying to play catch-up, learning the rules of the road to grasp all the "right" things to do and provide for my children's present stages and future successes. Maybe I was a real-life zombie? The body was carrying on, but the sleep-deprived brain… MIA?

Implanted into my thinking was this idea that it was

so important to make sure I got it right for my children. I became convinced there was only one shot at this: Only one stage of potty-training timing to get it done properly or "they say" there are psychological implications. Only one first day of school and making friends in that class. I had to be sure to guide them effectively so they were not dubbed the nerd, the one forever remembered in kindergarten due to legendary scenarios such as peeing their pants, eating their boogers, sniffing glue, etc. I had said from the beginning that I was going to dominate this job and be a success, and not lose myself, either. So, I resolved to learn how to get it right, not mess up, and give my kids the best shot in life. Maybe other moms with older kids and those who seemed to have it together, would have some answers?

Judgment Daze

Talking with and observing parents at school, playgroups, etc., I took renewed notice in what they talked about and how they did things. I soon learned much more about judgment and mom-shaming. Even among each other. I thought I would find some answers, but more often than not I heard how "so and so" was wrong to let her kids eat candy and how another mom believed in spanking and, gasp, this other mom allowed her kids to watch TV, even, SpongeBob! Another common denominator I noticed included self-negativity, mom's believing they were not enough to manage all of the demands they faced. And not feeling free to talk about it with the "you have all the time in the world to deal with everything" expectations. I realized I was certainly dabbling in that as well. Choosing to be a stay-at-home mom meant, I should have been able to handle all of this.

You know, I was trying to "mom-up", but the condescension for the stay-at-home mom also became more challenging and surprisingly more frequent. Although sometimes unintended, painful jabs at my chosen profession seemed "okay" to just blurt out, even from fellow moms. I subliminally and unintentionally took on all the wrong messages about stay-at-homers. My inadequacy was alive and well and growing like the blob. Triggering scenarios such as blatant speculation about "what I did all day", the competitive nature of some, the complete cluelessness of others, with the corrosive condescension of it all, sadly, seeped into my thinking without much evaluation. I battled with the seemingly phony, often repeated, saying about being a mother: "It's the most important job in the world." But it wasn't really respected. Like that's what the PC police dictated had to be said. Some didn't even get *that* memo.

One time I was chatting at a party with a couple and enjoying a discussion of current events and the latest in their world of the performing arts. After engaging with them for at least a half hour, connecting, and having a good conversation, they asked me the fatal, "And what do you do?" I replied, "I'm a stay-at-home mom and, basically, a professional volunteer." I wish there would have been a hidden camera. You would not believe how fast they whirled their heads around trying to find a reason to talk to someone else. I felt an urge to follow them and list off all the places I volunteered and what I did to make the world a better place… "It's unpaid, right, but really I do good things… and… wait up!" I'm pretty sure I saw them leave in neck braces from all the whiplash.

Unfortunately, I experienced many of these encounters. For instance, if I was at a gathering and it was a Saturday before a Monday holiday (Labor Day, Memorial Day, etc.), everyone would go around and say whether they were working or not on Monday, but they wouldn't ask me. I felt like I wanted to firmly add in, "YES, and when am I NOT working?" (And are you done with that plate so I can clear it and get the dessert?) But the validation seemed to never be there for the "most important job in the world". Coupled with the guilt of possibly screwing it all up, noticeably missing in these conversations was a discussion on things like work/ life balance even though that was discussed all the time in other professions.

If I mentioned I was hoping to change it up and leave the kids with EJ, there were questions like, "Why would you need to have a break?" implying my daily life is a break. I quickly learned it was important to not appear as if I was complaining about "my life of ease". For the record, as a stay-at-home parent, I did have the freedom to manage my days at home, the only problem being that the kids were always there, too, and very much dictating most of my daily tasks according to their needs. Always there. Follow-you-into-the-bathroom type of always.

Getting it right meant being on time, all systems go. How hard can that be day after day? I wanted to appeal to the "judges" and see if being on time just one day a week could count as impressive? Slightly approved?

At one point, I went to a group that was perfect for moms with young children. They discussed timely topics. There were moms with kids at the same stage, and the group provided regular support. Yet one thing stuck out to me: they tended to give a door prize to the first mom there. I always thought the prize should have gone to the last mom to get there, arriving in her pajamas not sure if she remembered all her kids or not. Perhaps she was even sitting in her car moments before, trying not to cry and debating whether to even go in because the get-together had started twenty minutes ago.

Ugh, being on time when no child around you has the same focus. Reminds me of a story. On one typical day for me, I had to get my oldest to the carefully chosen school, early. I was driving the carpool that day and my husband was out of town. I was feeling good, totally on the money timewise, with getting all of my kids in the car and still being able to pick up the other two kids in the neighborhood. There was no time to spare, and always lurking in the back of my mind was that feared call from the other moms about being late and making everyone late. But this day we were in good shape.

As I put the baby in the car seat, I heard that sound—the sound that has the power to strike fear in the hearts of mom-kind the world over. That explosive, intense, gurgly, squishy sound of a massive blowout. Seeing tsunami levels oozing out of the diaper and up her back, I realized this was going to be no quick fix. It was all-out panic and took me instantly to Defcon 1. I would need a new set of clothes for her (is the laundry dry yet?). I'd need a towel to cover the car seat—no time to clean it up. Which meant gag smell for the duration of the drive.

My oldest saw what was happening (or smelled, how could you miss it?) and suddenly got anxious to get to school on time. But just then, through his air-gacking, he remembered he needed a note signed for the teacher. Like right then. Which triggered my other child to remind me that he'd told the soccer coach we would bring snacks for the team today after school. As my head was spinning and slimy poop was embedding itself into my fingernails, my phone rang. Oh, no! The displeased moms from the carpool? Am I late?? No, it was my husband just finishing up his room service breakfast and wanting to wish everyone a good day. No one could hear him very well on speaker phone with all the crying. I think the baby might have been too. I got a text thirty minutes later from him: "Hang in there." So, I did. (My kids hilariously refer to these types of memorable incidences as "Poo-mageddon.")

Why in these moments did I tend to personalize this, put it on myself, making it my fault for not being perfect enough? Or even just enough? Couldn't I simply get a few kids to class on time? Was I that lame at an apparently piece-of-cake job? What has happened to me?

I felt plagued with so many expectations, like this unwritten thing about showing up at school with the "perfect cupcake"—that ultimate symbol of mom togetherness. The oooh and ahhh factor. One time it was my turn to be the treat provider (yes, I had knowingly signed up). I felt some pretty clear "guidance" (eyebrows lifted and heads tilted) that I must show up with the perfect cupcake: on time, no evil ingredients, store-bought only (like they never sneeze into the batter at a store), with occasion appropriateness (a Halloween cupcake for a birthday celebration? What the heck?), with well-managed contingencies for all possible culinary conflicts. There was some angst to get that right. I wanted each child to be able to partake with the class but didn't want to send anyone into anaphylactic shock.

The big day arrived, and after my careful planning, I think I scored a 5 out of 10 (points off for not having enough for all siblings that arrived unannounced that day).

Another time, one year for Halloween, I brought the

cupcakes and just taped about twenty boxes of chewable benadryl and an epi-pen to my clothes so that if anything I brought could affect someone in any possible way, it could be quickly handled. My worry went undiscovered, everyone just thought I was dressed up as a doctor, phlebotomist, or drug dealer for Halloween.

This nagging judgment we parents foist on each other was around every corner, and, alas, I had slipped into it too. Ugh. How? Well, at some point you must be a Room Mom because you need to be involved, put together the class parties, make awesome experiences for the kids, and (stealthily) observe how your kid is doing in the thick of it all. Well, "good" moms do that anyway. The ones that fit in, are judged approved and get head nods for organizational skills. And some validation.

So, I and a few other awesome moms put together the winter party for the kindergarten class. It's that fun party for kids right around Christmas in the winter. I found I had a little different philosophy in that it should be totally fun. I wasn't interested in a lot of sit down and follow directions and produce stuff. That's what normal school is for, right? Well, there was another mom who insisted on the kids sitting down and doing a craft that required several steps.

Although seemingly well intentioned to provide a craft, I and two others on the very important winter party committee said let's pass on that, okay? We've got games, snacks, songs, delicious chaos, and so forth. That mom seemed miffed but dropped it. Until the day of the party. In the middle of all the activity (three groups of kids were making a "snowman" of another classmate by teepeeing them), this same mom, instructed the class to get to their seats for a craft. I looked at her like, what the...? The other moms looked at me like, really? She proceeded to explain what to do and how to walk through each step, and the kids (hopped up on sugar by this point) looked like they couldn't even stay seated let alone follow directions. They were five and six years old.

It was really bizarre and ill-advised. No big deal in a way, but not the plan. What was the point in hijacking the festivities? So, I did the mature balanced thing and just asked her what was up and why did she decide to do that? We could have discussed it more if it was that important to her. Okay, not really. I wish. I was a caddy jerk and added to the judgy mom-versation after that party. We concluded she was insane, control-freaked, and out-of-line. Which is what it seemed, but I didn't really know why, or what could be going on with her. Maybe there was some good reason she felt this was important. Maybe her child felt the season's joy only through making a popsicle-stick Santa.

This was kindergarten, too—if none of these families moved, we would all be seeing each other at events all the way through high school. Great. The "can't beat 'em, join 'em" judgy conversation just felt awful. After all, she was a fellow mom, doing her best, too.

All this judgment swirling around from others, heaping on my own self-judgment and starting to join in toward others as well, was not good. I mean, this stuff hurts and leaves a mark.

Then I experienced a particularly painful incident. We had some friends over who were considering moving to another state for the wife's career. They were opening up and ruminating over the possibilities about what this move would look like for each of them and their children. We had moved plenty and had that perspective of starting over.

Working hard not to notice the lack of eye contact with

me in this conversation (the one who made it all happen "on the ground" of every move but what-evs), I remained fully engaged in the chat. The husband faced the prospect of starting over because his career and company would not transfer to this new location. That's when it hit. The comment that I wish I'd never noticed and have worked hard to forget. But I haven't.

He said, "Maybe I could just stay home with the kids and do nothing, you know, like Lynn."

Ouch. Dagger to the heart. This is why we don't run with scissors. Someone could get hurt. Surely, he could have misspoke. But that nugget of truth for him just lingered. In my wallowing, it felt like that was the actual truth of how everyone saw it. And sadly, I drank the Kool-Aid and believed the mom job was "nothing" and marginalized. Why was I such a weenie to let this not only bother me but fester? Why was I beating myself up and calling myself names about it too?

I stubbornly insisted on sticking with trying to do the best job possible, even though I was starting to seriously doubt myself. I succumbed to autopilot to have a better chance at raising my kids right, with all the right activities, so they could be successful. That's what seemed so much more important now, while the original idea of focusing on the moments got buried deep inside me. Controlling and planning the next and future moments ruled my thinking.

The kids liked what they liked, though. So, we fell into patterns, like chasing sports. How? By being completely available for each and every moment the coach created a practice, outing, event, or extra practice (for those who were "serious"). Be at everything, be available and coachable (and good), and you will play.

At one point, the coaches had spent more time with my children than I had. I was thinking about consulting them on my kids' strengths and what colleges they should consider. Or maybe they could get them to clean their rooms? Throw a few dishes in the dishwasher? Boiling it down, though, sports were a way for my kids to fulfill their need to fit in, and it was as strong as mine. So, I felt I had to support all of us in the over-scheduled quest for that.

We were all just doing our best, as best we knew anyway, trying to get it "right". Kids were to show up, play hard, be a good teammate; parents were to properly yell at umps and refs and harshly judge the opponent's questionable intentions (while cheering for them because we all signed that agreement to support the opponent, right?), and, of course, question the heck out of what the coach was thinking. Often the hardest part of some of that (besides screaming babies waiting for the hour-long epic post-game coaches' speeches) was the out-loud judgment and evaluation of the players (yes, kids) by other parents. It was bad enough to rip on their own kid in front of others, but when did it become okay to judge and rip on other children? One lovely experience even included seven-year-old girls playing soccer. Seven. Wish I could unhear that. Ugh, judgment.

Embracing Conformity

I remember one New Year kicking off and, as always, all the TV shows were focused on goals and resolutions. So exhausted from the big Christmas "show", New Year's party, and a house that still desperately needed to be cleaned up, I sat down and cried—that real cry, the victimy, hopeless sob. Why bother making goals for myself? What's the point?

The needs of this family and each individual will come first. Even worse, this was of my own making. I had pigeonholed myself, always putting everyone else's needs and issues before mine. It was way more than a bad habit, it had become my way of life. I remember that feeling of defeat on day one of that brand new year and not having a clue as to how to change it.

Granted, it was (or wasn't?) a first-world problem, no delusions there. But when you see yourself as stuck, you are stuck. Possibilities were limited. I wondered if others who seemed to have different circumstances or appeared to show up in certain ways were living their own "stuck" behind their own masks? And why were those masks more put together than mine? More sparkly?

I felt so truly grateful, and was told often how I should be so grateful for the choice to stay at home. AND I silently felt stuck on the hamster wheel of how this culture pictures the role of mom, buying into it fully as to not fail my children, making irreparable lifelong mistakes, but ignoring myself in the process.

So, I doubled down, just kept trying to measure up. I had absorbed plenty of the messages from the culture around me and the stealth parental programming that I was infused with, such as the acceptable ways to get an approval rating, the perfection required, the rules of the road of what's expected, especially from moms.

I learned it's about how your kids need to show up, analyzing what school to attend, what activities they need to do, like sports, piano, STEM, and so on, in order to grow up "properly". And if I did it right, they'd have a chance at success. It was entirely up to me to figure out how and what they should be doing and get it scheduled (you know, uniforms and equipment and five vegetables... then teach them to be great test-takers, and great toy-sharers and, and, and...) so, ultimately, you mitigate the disaster of them going down the wrong path.

But how did I know what the right and wrong paths were? Was there really a formula? Isn't each kid an individual human, and maybe I should see where their individual interests lie? I was just expected to figure it out, or I was already supposed to know, 'cause, like, I'm the mom. It would be clear, though, if I didn't get it right. For example, no piano lessons? Clearly that kid's brain will not fully develop, and forget any hopes of advanced math. College could be out. Doesn't matter that they are still in preschool. Doesn't matter that they really didn't like lessons and put peanut butter in the car ignition to avoid going. The paradox was that I should already somehow know everything to do at all times, and it had to fit in nicely with the expectations of this culture. So, I would be judged as approved. Good mom. (Sit, stay, roll over.)

Lost in the Fog

Maybe it's odd but I love fog. It's so totally cool. It surrounds you, envelops you, and has a strange comforting feel. You can see only your immediate surroundings with clarity. Whatever is directly right there in front of you, you can see clearly. You are present to the present. And it is beautiful. Maybe even more so than when the fog is lifted because then there is so much more to compete for your attention, and the beauty in front of you gets diluted through competition. In a heavy fog, you look around and you can't see much as you're guessing what's happening next. Prepare for it? Nope. Is it good or bad? What's that around the corner? Don't know. That uncertainty is the very uncomfortable part of fog. Who wants to pull out in front of a semi-truck you didn't see?

For me, it was being in the fog all the while hearing the messages of how I no longer measured up, just beyond what I could see clearly. What's worse? I listened. My lack of awareness and putting me on hold allowed that message to *take* hold.

I don't think it was just one moment, but I did fall asleep at the wheel of me. I had jumped into the deep end, that bottomless pool of expectations concerning the role of mom, and then soldiered through it in the quest to do my best for all. That fog, although it could be so cool, hadn't lifted.

And then… a light at the end of the tunnel pierced through the fog. My youngest was rounding the corner toward first grade. Full-day school! I had been a stay-at-home mom for twelve years. Dare I… create some next steps for… ME? Think of options, opportunities, new frontiers? What are my options? I always wanted to be an EMT—is it too late, I asked myself? What could that look like? What about my creativity? I love helping people and businesses with promotions, ideas, looking at what they are not looking at—a marketing solutionist maybe? Would anyone value my skill set? Do I still have a skill set? Where do I start?

Exciting and new possibilities were right around the corner. Surely my huge list of volunteering, organizing events, and fund-raising would be valued. Right? Either way, the welcomed thought process of reinventing myself had begun. I could surely figure out how to integrate a new job with my current job. I realized how I was so ready… ready to find myself again.

Wait... What?

As my mind continued to think about the next stage of possibilities for me (who?), I thought I would get my house in order. Or at least my "downstairs". I had some things going on with my health: specifically, some "functioning" that needed attention.

It turns out it was collective damage: The first baby paved the way with more than normal scar tissue from excessive stitches. The second little love was not so little. And the third little sweet pea—well, why not add to the interesting changes of motherhood? I discovered through some unpleasant symptoms that my girl stuff was out of whack and needed some support. I went to my OB/GYN, and he sent me to a specialist in my area. At least I knew I wasn't alone. If they have several doctors and it's a specialty, well, then, it's normal, right?

This guy made me feel really uncomfortable. He talked

about a slight prolapse of the uterus and how over time it would be worse and problematic, and he should just remove it right away (made me feel like he was already looking at a new Mercedes). Because he gave me the creeps, and I wasn't sure about just yanking stuff out, I tried another doc. This one wasn't creepy at all but also started saying I could remove the uterus because it may be prolapsing, and eventually I would have to remove it anyway. I just had a gut feeling that I didn't need to start removing stuff based on a "maybe" or a "might be". Doesn't a whole bunch of new shifting have to go on if a piece of the puzzle is now missing? You take something from your car, like a wheel, and I'm pretty sure it functions differently. It's wobbly, out of alignment. But these were the specialists.

I then talked with some different doctors to address this common problem. Different picture! They had a procedure to add support and stop the issues. Hmm. So, after talking to my husband and my mom ('cause she also had firsthand experience, and moms are automatically experts—it's required of the job), I decided to do the surgery to put stuff back where it belonged, the goal being to at least try to sneeze fearlessly.

For these particular surgeries, the doctor goes over with you how it's basically an art, not a science. Like they have to really try to figure out how to place the support material in the tissue, and it has to be the right support—not too tight and not too loose. I didn't envy him. Or me. I remember kind of joking—don't make it too tight and cause backup problems. Kind of afraid of that. But if you want to tighten the tummy, let's talk.

After the first surgery, you guessed it, it was too loose. So, they had to schedule a second round. Oh goody. More recovery, down time, and, you know, the other restrictions. Like don't you love it when the doctor tells you to take it real easy, stay sedentary, low stress. Does that come with a prescription for a nanny? Anyway, I scheduled the date for the second surgery in early January. With these surgeries came a six-week postoperative "husband restriction". Yes, a kiss good night and a hearty handshake is it. Knowing that this would be our lot for a bit, the night before, we decided we were going to "Netflix and chill". Wink, wink.

We had to be in Denver by 7 a.m., and the surgery was scheduled for 8 a.m. This was at least an hour drive from our home. I had followed all their instructions and answered yes, I was fasting; yes, I hadn't taken any medicines; no, I was not sick or had the flu; no, it was impossible to be pregnant. I kind of wondered in my head, would they be able to tell I got busy last night? No, impossible (right?). What did it matter? They didn't even ask that question, when was the last time… so guess that didn't matter.

So, fast-forward through healing and being a good girl for six weeks, and I'm at my post-surgery appointment in Denver. I had some things going on and a list of questions for the doc. This. That. And, oh yeah, being a very regular, set-your-calendar-by-me kind of gal, would there be any reason I would be late getting my period from this surgery? I'm sure the surgery would impact that, right? Probably would cause you to be a few months off for sure… um… right?

There was this strange nervous energy for both the doctor and me. A pregnant pause. We had one of those awkward sixth-grade giggle moments. The unsaid, "Like, uh, yeah, if you had sex and made a baby, you would be a bit late with your period." But I quickly reminded the doc my husband had had a vasectomy five-and-a-half years prior so a pregnancy wasn't possible. He had THE snip. I was even there at the vasectomy procedure as a material witness. I saw it. I saw the material. Others saw it. It surely was documented in a medical chart. I've been un-impregnated for five-and-a-half years, for goodness sake. Why was I building a case of proof or an argument that it couldn't be?

I had informed Mr. Doctorpants that it clearly wasn't possible, so what else is up? He mumbled incoherently, like to himself, and then, like in any good movie shot, he turned to the camera for a closeup and said, ominously, "If you are in fact pregnant, be sure to have a C-section or you will seriously damage what we have repaired and quite possibly impair your functioning for life." Oh, just that? Got it.

Wait, what's that supposed to mean? Are you talking the bag deal?

Oh, silly dude. He's a repair dude, NOT a reproduction dude, I reasoned. Phew.

We finished the post-op with all the questions and tests, and I was on my way. I proceeded to my car and began the long drive home. But I cannot say I was really present in my body. I had a super floaty feeling. That fog feeling set in. Like I wasn't really part of what was happening around me or what I was actively doing (driving!). Note to self, actually to us all, be sure to be patient and merciful to drivers around us, you never know what they may be going through.

Managing at least some safe driving skills, evidenced by no crashes or close calls (that I know of), I started going through a list of things in my mind—an honest look at some body symptoms I just attributed to this surgery, now six weeks ago. Things that I noticed in the early stages of my pregnancies every single time:

- sore tatas
- spacey
- tired
- frequent potty stops
- nausea
- sinus infection

Especially the last one. I seem to always get a sinus infection in the first trimester of my pregnancies. That one put me over the edge. My sinuses had been feeling terrible and getting worse. But it was January and with the weather and the lady who sneezed on me last week... again, building a case.

The more I drove the more I thought, well, maybe? Followed by, that's insane and impossible! What am I, Mother Mary here? Certainly not. A mind tsunami ensued.

Driving myself crazy and somehow closer to my home, I pulled off the highway to a handy-dandy Target. On a completely insane, waste-of-money impulse, I purchased the cheapest possible pregnancy test and went into the handy-dandy private restroom adjacent to the pharmacy and let it rip. Can you believe it? I got the only defective test on the shelf! It actually showed two blue lines, which would indicate a positive result! Tossed that puppy straight into the garbage can. I mean, really, I was mad at myself for wasting the money.

Then, sheepishly (as if someone were watching), I fished it out and threw it into my purse. Why? No idea. No rational reason, just did. I was still experiencing out-of-body issues. Don't judge.

Speaking of judging, as I came out of the restroom, a crowd of people had gathered. One older lady pointed and elbowed her friend: "Yep, I could tell a mile away, she's knocked up." Someone else said, "Duh, look at all the symptoms she's denying." So, I immediately defended myself and made a clear case that it was physically not possible, my husband had a vasectomy, he'd been tested AND free and clear for FIVE-and-a-HALF-years! They all laughed and said good luck with that. I also may have seen, out of the corner of my eye, some pigs flying and hell freezing over. Okay, so that didn't exactly happen. One lady just looked up as she was waiting for the bathroom.

Still dazed, I left Target as quickly as possible before someone wanted to do a price check and discover what I had just purchased.

I had an uber-surreal drive the rest of the way home. Now I had proof. Two blue lines. But the test was defective. I guess I could take another test? *No, this is ridiculous, remember,* I said to myself—*it's actually not possible.* Spending money on a new test is a total waste. But the other symptoms, sore breasts, tired, my eighth potty stop… still, really, what does that prove? But the dang two blue lines. Of a defective test. I was quickly driving myself crazy. And my new best friend was moving in too: denial. Little did I know we would be inseparable in the next few trimesters.

What's Real?

After a brief stop at home, I went to my next doctor appointment, which had been lined up for this same day, with my primary care doctor. I suspected I had a sinus infection, which of course, I did. At least that's not usually one of my indicators in the three previous pregnancies. Oh, wait…

I got to her office and waited after check-in, still stunned, naturally. I picked up a magazine and stared at it. I decided I was completely insane and needed to calm down. The waiting room was relatively quiet, just one other woman with her baby. I tried to read an article about being some sort of organized mom. After a little while, they called my name ("Denial? Denial Bodnar?"), a name I recognized, so I decided to get up and go back with the nurse.

We started with the usual weigh-in with the shoes off. Normally you notice the results of the mood-maker (scale), but the numbers didn't even register. I got into the exam room, and, after a bit, my sweet doctor came in with her usual calm, happy, positive greeting. As if nothing were upside down in the world. I told her about my sinus symptoms, the length of time, and so on. She did her exam— you know, the eyes, ears, nose, throat, listening to my chest and my breathing. She concluded it was definitely a sinus infection and said I needed to get on antibiotics. And there you have it.

As a footnote, I said to her, "Strangest thing happened today." She's like, oh, do tell. "Well," I said, "I took a test, a pregnancy test, a little while ago, and I got a positive result. Now, I'm quite certain it's defective, of course, because of EJ's vasectomy five-and-a-half-years ago. But isn't that really weird?" She, with a little too much gleam in her eye, jumped up and said we'd better take a pregnancy test immediately to be sure. In my head I was like, *Isn't that overkill? You heard me say defective.* So, she set me up with the perfectly sterile collection cup, reminded me of the instructions on collecting a proper sample (instructions that I could say in my sleep and in German), and sent me off to the doctor's office loo. I dutifully followed the instructions so that the negative result could not be questioned due to a faulty procedure. I placed the sample in the little cubby box thingy with a door through to the other side of the wall. I imagined some thrilled lab tech back there going yay! more pee—pick me!! I washed my hands and with a very nervous, butterfly-filled stomach, returned to the exam room.

Five hours later she bounded back into the room. Okay, it was only like ten minutes, but it seemed longer. She bubbled out, "You are very pregnant—it was positive!" I'm like, wait… waaa… what? What do you mean by very pregnant? I'm imagining hyped-up levels of HCG and that she already knows it's twins or something. Like I'm over forty and more eggs are making a run for it each monthly ovulation, and since twins are in my family history, the chances of that happening to me could increase, and, and, and… She says no, it's just that the pregnancy test results left no room for question—it was a definite positive result. I was pregnant. For real. Boom.

I sat there motionless, and I didn't feel like I could process actual speech for a long time. It must not have been that long because she was still there looking at me. I started incoherently saying, "But I'm almost forty-three years old. I'm already blessed with my children and was done. My husband had a vasectomy. And yes, he did all the post-vasectomy tests and no worries. No evidence. No swimmers. We've been going for five-and-a-half years without another thought. How could this be? I don't have any more baby things, everything is gone. I can't do sleepless nights. My body, the surgery—this may be a no-return situation."

I started crying uncontrollably.

She gave me a big hug, so sweet and kind, and said it would be wonderful. It may be shocking right now, understandably, but it will be absolutely beautiful. She continued, "I secretly wish my husband's vasectomy would fail. I would LOVE to be finding out I was pregnant even at this age" (I believe we were about the same age).

I looked at her like she had just grown wings and was sprinkling fairy dust. Denial can cause hallucinations, I have discovered. I mean seriously. This news just completely changed my life in ways I could only think about and in other ways I had no way of comprehending. In that moment, though, I felt a pervasive cloud of "stuckness" like a shadow over me that settled in for the long haul.

She made sure I was okay and able to put one foot in front of the other to walk out the door. She told me to call my OB/GYN immediately. For the driving home part, I was on my own. And you already get how that goes. Did I mention we should all have mercy on fellow drivers who seem to not be fully there? You may never know what's going on in their world. Strongly recommend mercy. You may need it someday, too.

The Reveal

Okay, so imagine the scene. I have had the morning visit with the surgeon, the drive home from Denver, the "false" positive pregnancy test, the "very" positive pregnancy test, and the sinus infection confirmation.

Let's be honest, my subconscious had known for some time too. It was just not allowed to speak up. So, even with my advanced stages of denial, I realized I was about six weeks with child. I entered my house. I heard my husband, who was in his home office working. I pictured it like this: two phones, one in each ear, him saying, "Buy, buy! Sell, sell!

Everyone's selling? Then buy!" That wasn't exactly it, but he was clearly in the throes of his day, on the phone, with deadlines and a look of focus.

I sat down on the couch and just stared at him. I think I must have looked eerie, like someone just bitten and about to turn zombie. He kind of stopped, held his hand over the phone, and mouthed, "You okay? Is something up?"

In that moment I had complete clarity. Telling him the not only unlikely but impossible would be cruel. I hesitated a little bit because it would've been kind of funny to watch him process it all in the moment, but in the end, I decided it would be better left until there were no distractions. And it would be a "day changer" to say the least. Like 7,665 days would be changed until the baby would be twenty-one years old. Massive delay in our parental graduation time-line. He will be sixty-six years old.

"Yes, I'm okay," I said. But not really.

Getting a sitter on short notice, I talked him into going out to dinner so we could "connect". (Although, isn't that how this whole thing started?). He was like, great, and good idea. Surely in his head he was thinking, yep, today's the day she's gone over the edge. She's acting so weird, out of body, not herself. Later, I would find out he was scared that there was really bad medical news from the doctor.

I got dinner started for the kids, homework under way, and most issues hopefully addressed for the moment. The sitter showed up, and off we went. I was very quiet on the drive over to the restaurant. It was close to our house, and he was chatting on about the day, goings-on at work, thoughts about things from his day. I was lost inside my head and suddenly realized I could have made a fun way to reveal the news. Like all the cool ways people reveal there is a baby on board. I could have been creative. Like giving him a bag of fertilizer and an egg and saying, "Guess what?" Or something with birds and bees. Or a "Father of the Year" mug. Or actually something really cute, like the positive pregnancy test in his cheeseburger or among his fries—actually laughed out loud on that one. Or asking how he would feel about a new puppy and going from there.

But I was too jacked up for the creativity thing. My head was spinning. Truly lost in a fog of what's real and what's not, my thoughts were a million miles away. Seriously, as in outside of our Milky Way, through a wormhole, a megabazillion miles away. As I was grappling to accept what was real and what was not, I almost had an uncontrollable laugh come over me. My gosh, his whole world was going to be completely blown away in a few moments.

Nobody had witnessed me walking through this day: Each step, each shocking moment. The weird exchange with the surgery doc. The certifiable denial. The moment of truth at Target. The shock and then the tears that shot horizontally straight out from my eyes at my primary care doctor's office. But now I was going to see every flinch in his expression, every movement of his body language, and of course, what he would say. Or not say (gulp). Maybe he'd faint? Maybe he'd freak? Should I be ready for that, too? What all should I be ready for?

We pulled into the parking lot of the restaurant, and he found a spot and parked. For some reason, I was looking to see if people were around, like they would overhear, but saw nobody. I said, "Okay, so let's stay in the car. You can unbuckle, but let's stay here for a minute."

He cautiously stuttered, "Okay… Are you okay? I mean, honestly, you are acting really weird and kind of scaring me."

I said yes, I'm okay, I think, revisiting in my mind whether he may want to actually fasten his seatbelt again, I took in

a large nervous breath. He was like seriously, what's up? I
briefly looked outside my window at the bright stars on this
frosty February night and took a deep breath. I don't think I
had ever known beforehand, with such clarity, that a moment
was about to happen that would change everything.

I started rambling like a chipmunk on speed, but not
really saying anything. Yep, voice went up a couple of octaves
and all. Read this next paragraph as fast as you can in a very
high voice without taking a breath like a hysterical rodent,
and you will get the idea:

"Well I don't know where to start or what to say but I
should have something cute and fun and creative but I don't
and you need to know this as soon as possible but it's crazy
and I'm not even sure if I grasp this and, uh, um, haha, like
so here's the thing I just can't even believe it and you are going
to freak out a little bit, but really it's okay and don't worry
it will also all be okay and we can handle anything together
of course, but this is really unexpected previously considered impossible and I don't even know how it's possible, but
life can be wild right? and, gosh I'm so nervous but"—He
sweetly and patiently put his hand on my arm and said,
"Lynn, please take a deep breath and just tell me what you
are talking about. You really ARE scaring me."

So, deep breath taken, I said, "So, here's the thing: we
are going to have a baby. I'm pregnant."

I felt so completely raw. Totally vulnerable. Not entirely
worried about his reacting badly, just feeling that this was
an ominous moment with the potential to obliterate me.
Didn't even venture to think what he would be thinking or
predict his response. It hadn't even remotely occurred to me
that he would think I had cheated, but what if he went with
that? But we had created a marriage of twenty years at this

point. We really didn't worry about that. But what if he did, and now I had to prove that's not the case on top of everything else? Which, for the record—this was not a case of needing a paternity test—would be a waste of money. Even the cheap one.

You have to wonder how he would be feeling at this moment. He was initially shocked by the news, of course. It was quite the info to process, and, really, how would anyone react? Check out his reaction:

After I finally got to the point, he looked at me for one second, put his hands on the steering wheel, and stared out into space. A nano-second later, literally, he said (and I will never, ever forget this), "Wow. Incredible. How did we get so lucky? God has blessed us again. He must think we are pretty good parents to make this happen for us again! What a blessing this is for us!"

I realized anything else would have trashed me. I just wanted this to be okay, and I didn't even know what okay looked like. I didn't want to have to take on any emotional train wreck from him because I was already a mess. Telling that story makes me cry to this day. It's tender and amazing, and I am so grateful he reacted that way—his clarity, faith, belief, and dedication to me. In real time, his response felt like the deepest possible unbreakable support, like from the core of the earth. I would certainly draw on this for the times to come.

Most people can't even believe that was his instantaneous response, right there in the moment. He was incredible—present and clear. It was so gracious and wonderful, and I believe divinely inspired. It was a beautiful gut reaction without any time to add thoughts to it, or reason. That would come later, like, another mouth to feed, college funds, how old will I be when she graduates from high school? We just hugged each other in the front seat of the car and cried and laughed. That was becoming a bit of a pattern for the day, with a weird, awkward out-of-body laugh.

So, we went inside the restaurant and worked on processing this together. Telling him and being able to talk about it was making it more real. How great it was to be in this together! We had eaten at this place many times, and when we were asked for our order and couldn't really communicate, they said they would get us what we usually ordered. Nice, because it was as if we had forgotten how to speak English. During dinner, it was humorous to me to watch him completely space out, then be jolted back into the room. I'd had all day to try to come to terms with this new reality. I comforted him by letting him know I had been on that same planet a bazillion miles away all day.

He was like, "Yeah! That's why you came into my office all Stepford-wife-like. You kind of scared me. I thought you had bad news about your post-op visit or a family member was diagnosed with something." I didn't want him to be scared but didn't have full control of my rational brain. Wow, claiming baby brain already.

Our dinner settled in, and we were just processing and talking. We looked around at other people dining and were cracking up over how much our world had changed with two simple blue lines. What was going on with everyone around us? Did they find out they were pregnant today? How many dudes sitting there had the snippage? How would they react if we just did the movie-style awkward stand-up-in-a-restaurant and announced, "We're having a baby!" And, "We thought it was impossible and have been free and clear for five-and-a-half-years, so, yeah." Breadstick drop.

What Now?

They asked if we wanted dessert, and we both laughed for some reason. I thought, yes, a full set of everything newborn that I have already given away would be perfect for dessert. Over dinner, EJ and I started talking about practical next steps, interlaced with how old he would be at various stages of this baby's life ("You know I'll be sixty-three-years-old when she graduates high school?"). We realized we had to think about how this would work. For example, how far along was I? I figured it was just going on seven weeks. Our standard operating procedure was not to say anything to anyone until after the three-month point. Having experienced two miscarriages before, it's really hard to tell family and friends and then have to talk to everyone about the loss when you aren't really ready to handle that yourself. And with this bombshell…

But, would we stick to the same strategy? And, oh, gosh, what about miscarriage odds for this little one? I had the two miscarriages in Germany, at a younger age, too. Also, we now had older kids who would need to find out first and from us, not overhear the big news from someone else—although it would have been so much easier to have someone else explain all this to them. We concluded that the best thing to do was not say anything to anyone. I would get an appointment with my OB/GYN and get some good info. Our kids would be clueless to the symptoms and probably not even notice the nausea, and if I went the route of vomiting, they would still never guess the reason (pull out the old "Zookeeper" game?). Adults—close friends—now that's another story. But, and you know how it goes at parties and stuff, people joke around, and everyone knew EJ was already "fixed". So, we had some cover, for a while anyway.

We finished up our dinner, time to get home. We walked to the car, and again, that weird, nervous giggle happened for both of us. For me, the fifth time that day.

Random thoughts and math equations. At least another eighteen months of being the designated driver. Add that on to the approximately sixty-two months already served (nine months of pregnancy + breastfeeding months × three kids).

So, now, just act normal. Right. The next day I worked really hard to get any sort of focus at all. I was in shock and denial. That denial would last for quite a while, I would find out. Literally, until labor started. What made it all the more difficult was that I'm a pretty transparent person. Normally, what you see is what you get. Hiding something this huge (and each month would be huge-r) was gonna be pretty hard for me. But again, first things first.

I anxiously called my OB doctor's office, and the scheduler said I would need to make an appointment at some point but would have to speak with the nurse first. I'm like, okay, is the nurse there? Nope, but she would give her a message and call me back. I would also be finding out that everything overwhelming would seem to take FOREVER. Two days later I got a call back:

"Hello, this is the nurse for your doctor. Is this Lynn?"

(My head said yes, I think, yes, it is, or at least I think so. I've lost myself lately. Maybe I should check the ID in my purse?)

"So, I understand you have had a positive pregnancy test?"

"Yes," I said. "And it comes as quite a shock. My husband had a vasectomy. FIVE-AND-A-HALF-YEARS AGO. You know, the permanent birth control. The one that you never think is possible to get pregnant with. The procedure that causes you to focus on your life, your children, your next steps and goals with no more baby stages. You know, that vasectomy."

"I see," she responded. "Well, what do you plan to do?"

I plan to make an appointment and get an idea of what I'm in store for with these new variables. "I need to make an appointment," I said.

She came back, "What do you plan to do?"

I was thinking, this is the part where you look at your schedule and the openings and I look at mine and we agree to a date and time. You know, an a-p-p-o-i-n-t-m-e-n-t.

"Yes, but what are your plans?"

Gosh dang, completely clueless. I was thinking I already had baby-brain because I did not understand. Maybe I should try it in German?

And then it finally hit me—she was asking if I was contemplating abortion, maybe adoption, or having the baby and keeping it.

Through all the shock, fear, denial, selfishness, physical detriment, body/health fears, and so much more—gotta say—never considered for one second not having this baby. Even with the concept being super new to my brain, and now EJ's brain, we never once pictured not having this little one in the new and expanded family picture. This was happening for a reason, although I certainly didn't know why. Plus, I might just miscarry anyway being so "old". The wait and see game. Suddenly I had a flashback to the woman I met years ago in the German doctor's office. It was such a distant memory, but I wondered about her. As I was comfortable with my own clarity in my situation, I sent her a little love all these years later.

So, the nurse made the appointment, in no particular hurry to have me seen. "Oh, how about in three to four weeks?" I'm like, I'm standing outside right now. But I asked why wait so long, and she indicated there was no rush to get in, and I should know with three other pregnancies what to expect in the next few weeks. I felt fairly hysterical—why am I not going to be seen right now?! But it was true, what was the rush? How many blue lines did I need to see to confirm this? I could also certainly do the math on a due date. I think I was looking to talk to someone who would maybe understand, hold my hand, comfort my fears? And then she reminded me to get a good prenatal vitamin, especially... wait for it... with my "advanced maternal age."

There it was. The first label to this situation. These three words would become one of those labels that even if you try to peel it off, it never goes away. Shards of it are left everywhere, never to be removed. Little did I know I would be hearing them over, and over, and over, and over, and over again. Instant grandma-hood. Look at the old lady having a baby. Isn't she old enough to have figured this out? Why is she risking this at such an advanced age? This was all happening in the mid-2000s when a baby at this age was rare. But, why couldn't the label be a bit kinder? Maybe, Fertile at 40+ or Mature Mother?

The appointment was set, and I felt like I was just sitting with my bewilderment and waiting and waiting. I'm not really sure what I was waiting for, just advice, or support, or understanding or comfort from the nurse or doctor because surely they would understand and have seen this before. I had certainly never heard of this happening before! I felt panicked and needy, but they would definitely help me sort this out. Help me make some sense of this, which I thought would be comforting.

We stuck with the plan to keep it to ourselves. Since EJ

mostly worked from home and we saw each other all day, we just kind of stared at each other and smiled and tried to grapple with the pregnancy being real.

We talked about a whole bunch of things, of course. He brought up the reminder of potential miscarriage, and we walked through that possibility together too. Not too deeply worried about it, just kind of, let's see what's meant to be. On my sickest days, with that down-and-out-all-alone feeling, I was like, fine, if miscarriage is what's going to happen anyway, then let's go. Throwing up sucks. It tethers you home and wipes you out.

Even still, it was hard to keep the news to myself. A girl also needs her girlfriends, especially for the ultimate girl-only experience of pregnancy and childbirth. Having EJ was key, don't get me wrong. I can't even imagine the long, lonely road of not having a solid partner during pregnancy, surprise or not. But I was finding that I needed my girlfriends. They would understand, support me, help me, appreciate the ins and outs (pun intended), and commiserate. Wouldn't they?

Conceive, Don't Grieve

I was sure I could talk to the doctor about this. He HAD to have seen this before, or helped women with unexpected pregnancies. He could help me understand what it would be like at forty-three years old—implications for my body, risks, and so on, right? He'd been an OB/GYN for like eighty years. Yep, couldn't wait to get to that appointment!

Finally, the appointment day came, and I went in. EJ wasn't available to go with me, and of course, it was no big deal to go by myself because I had done that a billion times before. So, I arrived, went through all the measurements and metrics, and sat in the room waiting for the doctor. He came in and said, "So, we have some new developments!" (We? Whatever.) I started explaining the whole situation. During my soliloquy, he said, "Oh, so an 'oops' baby." I immediately corrected him and eventually found that I would say this a million more times in my life: "No. This is a bonus baby." Clearly with this miracle, God sent this one to us to be part of our family plan. Thanks to my wonderful mother-in-law, who had eleven children (planned on eight but had three more), I learned the term bonus baby. She insisted on that term for her additional three babies and often told the story about how important that wording was. Couldn't have agreed more. So thankful to have learned that from her, not even knowing how important it would be for me personally. Also, my husband was a bonus baby (number nine of the eleven)!

As I was continuing to process my situation with the doctor, I just started to sob. I guess it all had built up waiting to talk with him. I tried to tell him how this was really changing things for me. How my youngest was going to start first grade in the fall, and I had dared to make some personal goals. How scared I was about the health and well-being of this baby, due to my age. And honestly, fearing whether I could handle this. The lack of sleep, the focus and energy needed, the fear of implications from the surgery I'd had, and would my boobs just plain fall off if I nursed a fourth child?

It came as quite a shock when he had no patience for my fears. He kind of listened and answered with a short, "It will be fine." He said although he didn't really know about all the potential damage with the transvaginal sling, we would work with the other doctor and do a C-section as recommended. It was especially stunning when he said, "Really, it's nothing to be so upset about. You should feel lucky you don't have cancer or something serious." Boom. The first painful slam about how I "should" feel. What I should be grateful for and how I'm lucky because it could be so much worse.

Over the years, doctors must hear and see it all. They may find it hard or lose patience to hear each person's issues and stories over and over again. He could have just given a diagnosis to another woman before me about having stage four cervical cancer. Or shared the news with someone about their breast cancer. Or told some little sweetheart that she would never conceive. I get that. But I really needed support for where I was mentally and emotionally in that moment. I went to him because he was so great in caring for me when I had just moved back to the states, pregnant with my daughter. But this time, I left the office devastated and had a good, long, lonely cry in my car. I was confused and it left me wondering, "Is it okay to feel how I feel?" And how *do* I feel? Does society get to dictate how I should feel and how to proceed? Is that what I'm being told now? I've never even heard of this happening before, but there are already "should's" on how to handle it?

My feelings were as crazy as my hormone levels. I was beginning to feel like I could only be painfully honest with myself. I was just really confused and supremely stunned on so many levels. I had no idea what was coming next, let alone how to be ready for it.

Gotta say, I was so clearly stuck with one overriding issue: unwavering denial. I just couldn't believe this was real. This was really happening. It was the only thing cresting the fog of my days, grasping the reality of it, and wrestling with the "fact" that it wasn't even possible. I was in denial until the day I went into labor. Not kidding.

Imagine the war going on inside my head. On one

hand, it is such a beautiful thing! A new baby, our family growing, the joy and wonder for us all. Kumbaya. But I just wasn't planning on it even being possible. Like a day comes along where you are not subject to gravity. How do you just manage and accept that? No big deal, just stuff floating everywhere. Just relax. Even though you were given no warning and had no idea it was remotely possible. It was just plain hard to wrap my head around. The deep confusion— and please be super clear on this—was about the detour to my life that I didn't expect or quite frankly want along with the physical fears. My mindset was that I was past a certain stage of raising small children and excited for the next stage. All in. Making family plans. And plans for ME! I hadn't done that in over a decade. So, the confusion was not wanting the DETOUR. I ALWAYS wanted the human, the child, the gift, and the blessing. The definition of MIRACLE. I never once thought about not wanting HER, I just struggled with the 180 degree change in my thinking and plans.

I struggled with the thought of starting over, on so many levels. Like my body. How do you bounce back from pregnancy at this age? My last baby was born when I was thirty-six, and things basically came back, but noticeably differently than they had at thirty-one with my firstborn: the weight gain, the "downstairs," the hormone fluctuations. Not to mention, what if carrying this baby would cause problems with my bladder and urethra and, seriously, maybe call for a bag situation for short or long term?! I was legit afraid of that. Actually, terrified. Who wouldn't be?

What is a C-section like? I know many friends have had one and been fine (and what was their age?), but what's that like to be cut open, haul out the goods, and sew all your layers back again? How can that be better or easier on the body?

What's the impact on the baby? Plus, I wouldn't get to work with the labor and delivery, work with my body and make it all happen. I pictured being drugged up (again) and just completely numbed and hearing the baby cry when they got it. Maybe not a big deal, and I was grateful for the medical advances to make this possible and be safe, but it just wasn't me. Made me feel like I'd be a bystander. But the risks were too great for that long-term damage, so I wasn't going to be stupid, either…

The massive fears in my head were about being older parents and having older DNA in the egg and sperm. We had all heard about older parents and the much higher rates of birth defects in their babies. So, I was thinking, this would be a massive redirect of my life with a new baby I didn't plan on and a stronger possibility of Down Syndrome or other things I didn't understand. How would I learn how to support a special needs child on top of it? Did you find out and get into support groups to teach you? Truly ignorant of what it would take to raise a special needs child and what the prospects were, I was swirling with the fear of my own inadequacies to handle this and the selfish thought that I just couldn't do it. I didn't know how. I didn't want to know how. I felt like I was barely treading water in a river swiftly heading for a waterfall.

And I was just plain done! I still would have to care for all the needs of the other three kids. They wouldn't get any less demanding—they would get more so, if anything. I worried about how exhausted I would be because I was already hanging on. I just couldn't visualize how to make all the moving parts come together. That was where I had let my situation get to. I was pretty good at being a stay-at-home mom with every detail and need managed, but I really was managing all the homestead and kid stuff single handedly. How did a newborn's "day in the life" fit in with the already over-scheduled older kids? 'Cause I was a good mom, making sure to get them to everything so they would have a chance to somehow thrive in this world. Now what? Would I have to choose whom to be a good mom to? Do you breastfeed while handing out the half-time snacks at soccer? Is that a thing? Or does that now get you registered as a sex offender?

The mistakes I made just taking care of everything for my family explained why I already expected to be so over-whelmed—why I felt so confused, in denial, and discouraged at starting all over. I did too much. I was under the influence of needing to have it perfect. I thought I could head problems off at the pass if I controlled the issues from the start. Now add the physical requirements of babies, the lack of sleep (again, my kryptonite), and the worries about handling the whole load, all while expecting myself to not miss a beat with the other kids. Because that's what would be expected of me, too.

I began to realize, as I journeyed through my brain that it would HAVE to look different. Some of the ridiculous perfectionism that wasn't good anyway would have to go.

But I had to recognize and see something before I could address it, deal with it, and decide what I would rather have it look like. There were just those nagging, ingrained expectations, that stay-at-home mom with "ease and endless time". No excuse to not get it perfect. I needed to figure out how to manage much better than I ever had before.

As the party of confusion, denial, discouragement, and lingering shock continued, the new center of attention emerging was the guilt, although that would seem like nothing when "judgment" and her sister "outright rudeness" crashed the party. I wish I would have known I needed a bouncer. Unprepared again.

Telling Others Was Really Telling

A couple of weeks later, I was signed up to go on the sixth-grade field trip with my oldest son's class to a museum. Mercifully, it was in town. Thinking that joining the kids on the bus would be a vomitorium waiting to happen, I opted to drive my car and meet the kids there. My friend had also signed up and said she would like to ride with me. Uh oh, alone in a car with my close friend. Be strong.

All was going pretty well. At the museum, the waves of nausea were brutal, but I kept deciding mind over matter, and I would be fine. Like it works that way. I caught myself eyeing each room we entered for a waste basket. Imagining a grab and run to the hallway to take care of business didn't really make me the best field trip mom that day. It struck me that on the inside (and desperately trying to keep it there), I was struggling, in turmoil, physically ill, and truly freaking out. And not one person around me knew. It makes you think—who else that day, or any day, is right next to you freaking out? About to lose it? So lonely in their problem that they are on the edge? And for whatever reason, unable to talk about it.

And, so, yeah, at one point I ran to the bathroom and horked. I was simply grateful it was in time. Just imagining my son's friends "mentioning" how his mom threw up on the skeleton display for years to come felt undignified and unfair to him. No one was in the bathroom either! So, my little secret was safe, right? Because you have to explain that stuff if someone is there. And my girlfriend would certainly have given me that look, after trying to explain that I probably had a random stomach upset... like, have you thought about... like, when was your last period?

In the car on the way home from the museum, which seemed like days later, she did say to me, "I don't want to pry or anything, but are you okay? Is something going on?" Dang. There goes my Academy Award for best actress. I cracked. I just started crying. Hard. Then she got worried. I said nothing was wrong, kind of. No serious illness. EJ, kids, parents, dog all okay. I just blurted out that somehow I was expecting. We just looked at each other and then bust out laughing as she said, "Somehow?" We talked for a while, and she was empathetic, amazed and freaked out. She encouraged me that all would be fine, and the blessing would be fantastic! She also said she was going to have her husband checked for swimmers the second it was possible (he was deployed overseas), but she was still very happy for me. This would be the first of so many different reactions. I never gave one thought to how people would react or what they might say. I was too wrapped up in myself.

Fessing up to EJ that I had told one of our friends, we

decided we had better come up with a "reveal" plan before things started revealing themselves. With the friend I told the news to, our boys were all best buds and hung out together. It was particularly important to tell our current three children about this news ourselves—very life changing for them as well. We kept thinking we just had to be the ones to tell them, in our own way and with the right timing (not just when heading to a soccer game, like, do you have your cleats? Water bottle? You're gonna have a brother or sister, shin guards?). At the time, our oldest was eleven years old, in sixth grade. Our second child was seven years old and in first grade. The youngest was five years old and in kindergarten. Just coming straight out with it was probably the best way, right? That's what it said in the book, *How to Tell Your Kids You Are Going to Have a Baby When They've Probably Heard You Were Done and "Couldn't"*.

There were big things to consider, like the youngest and the only girl losing that status. There would be a new "baby". With any news, I have found over the years, and with kids especially, it's about the bottom line of what it means for them and their way of life—any moves, family decisions, new chore charts, or other kind of big stuff, like another person joining the family.

The Kids

We gathered the kids around in our office and closed the door (not sure why, everyone was there) and had everyone take a seat. The oldest had a serious look on his face. He may have been expecting the worst but hoping for a family discussion on where to go for vacation. The seven-year-old was blissfully clueless. A second dog maybe? Just along for the ride. The "baby" girl just hung out like kindergarteners do looking for something to draw on or fidget with. We looked at each other, not having really rehearsed anything, and just kind of went for it.

"So, kids, we wanted to let you know about some exciting news" (read "we are setting the stage and telling you 'this is great!'").

"I'm going to be having a baby in the fall. A baby is growing in my tummy right now, a brother or sister for you all" (read "holy wow—did I just say that out loud? Is it real?"). I reminded myself that however they reacted, they were kids. Whatever they said, don't cry.

EJ said, "So, what do you kids think?"

Chirp, chirp.

Now, in all fairness, they were at various stages of their comprehension of the birds and the bees. The oldest, in his logical, methodical young mind, needed to understand about how babies were made when he was five years old.

Back when I was pregnant with my third, I picked him up from school one day and took him out for a doughnut. He began asking questions about the baby in my tummy. I have always told my kids, I will answer any question you ask me to the best of my ability. Chomping on the iced chocolate doughnut, he asked how the baby got in there. I delicately told him it takes a sperm and an egg that come together, God puts in the soul, and a baby grows in the mommy's tummy. Right. Good. Well said, ol' girl.

Not satisfied, he clarified, "So Daddy has the sperm part and Mommy has the egg part? But HOW do they get together? WHEN?" he asked. Resisting the temptation to say, "When the kids are finally asleep and no one has a headache, or definitely after a few gin and tonics," I told him when the mom and dad love each other so much they get close and hug and, yeah, love each other closely (I really should have read the book on this, thought there was more time).

He shot back if hugging each other is close enough for the sperm and egg to get together, where are they each from? This kid was not going to quit. Fasten your seatbelt, son. So, then when the mom and dad love each other, often times get married, get close, hug each other, love each other so much, and are even close enough where the penis and the vajayjay are together, the egg and sperm have a way to join up and then stay with the woman and grow in her tummy to make a full baby. "Oh," he said. "One more question" (are you kidding me?!?!), "can I have another doughnut?" YES— as I jumped up and ran to get him a doughnut and me off the witness stand.

My second oldest had some of the talk, but no interest to pursue the details. He was still pretty young for it. He would be on the slow and steady introduction plan over time. My daughter at five years old had just random little hints at info via playing with Barbies—perhaps a similar amount of information as my introduction to the subject as a kid from my mom via how our teddy bear hamsters "played." At any rate, it was important to know the stage they were each at and where their minds would go—and most importantly, that none of them would really understand how much life as they knew it would change. Including me.

Over the next week, finding out how we were very surprised to be having a baby, my oldest would ask us more questions (predictable). How could we be surprised? Knowing how babies are made in more detail since the doughnut discussion several years before, he knew we would have to know that we did "THAT". And, therefore, knowing we did THAT, we would logically know we would have a baby. It was really hard not to bust out laughing as we literally watched it dawn on him that people do THAT for the sake of doing THAT, not ONLY to make a baby. Wish I had videoed that little moment. Gem.

The other two, being younger, just went along with it. Like follow the leader. They watched their older brother and followed our lead, seeing it as a good thing. Thank goodness, because along with the denial, I was starting to feel so many things. I felt blessed, of course. That's how I was supposed to feel. Slap on my excitement between trips to the bathroom and smile. But then add other guilt-ridden, not "acceptable", fearful and selfish things going on in my head that I also felt I couldn't share. Too vulnerable. Too embarrassing. Too ungrateful. Too shameful. These included thoughts like, what about my hopeful and excited, long-awaited-for next steps? New goals? Next phase? And how many more years of parenting judgment from others now? What's going to happen with my body? Will it be okay? Will the C-section avoid the complications from the other surgery? Or…?

Some serious feelings of loneliness set in, even though I was surrounded by people. It's pretty hard to punch yourself in the face, but I was beating myself up like a prize fighter, creating a whole new level of mom guilt.

The Friendlies

So, at this point, our kids knew we were going to have another baby in October. My field trip friend knew but hadn't said a word to anyone. She stopped by one day, and her husband happened to call from his deployment in Afghanistan. On speaker phone, EJ said we had some news to share—guess what it is? Somehow, he guessed I was pregnant! I was beyond stunned. He and EJ immediately carried on about how amazing *EJ* is. (And he is, but seriously?!) "Can't keep a good man down," EJ crowed. His chest gained about eight inches that day alone. Interesting to observe. It truly was funny stuff with the obvious jokes about EJ's superman abilities. I noticed my girlfriend saying, "Isn't this all great? How exciting that WE are having a baby!" It felt so encouraging in that moment. Also, quite noticeable was her little comment (with a ventriloquist's smile), "As soon as you get home, let's get you into the urologist, honey!" Made sense to me of course but... did I have some disease?

Off to another family friend's house. We asked them if we could come over to share some news. The guy thought we were moving to China. The wife (and my buddy) blurted out, "You're pregnant," for her guess. Risky, but accurate! How were these people guessing this? I still wasn't even sure it was true. With their usual warmth and encouragement, their kind support was there. The next set of friends responded similarly: "Congrats! Great news!! (And that out-of-the-side-of-the-mouth nudge, "Hey, sweetie, get yourself checked next week, okay?" that I would overhear yet again). I was starting to feel contagious. And oversensitive. The simple congratulations and gracious reception of the news from our initial sharing with good friends was much appreciated, as I would find out.

I was gathering that I would need to handle this graciously and with calm acceptance. I had started to get the feeling that's what was "expected" with this unexpected situation. This was my filter, my lens, and how it seemed I had to start dealing with this—more alone in my true feelings and certainly not expressing them. It's not like I was all negative, but, candidly and painfully, I admit that I was really struggling with how to put meaning to all my feelings. Allowing guilt to reign instead of being okay with how difficult this was for me.

Deluged with unprocessed emotions and getting initial responses from people who treated it as great news, there was no room to talk about or work through my raw emotions of denial, and how I didn't want the huge life/ body/responsibility/timing changes. I started to feel really alone. Who could I talk to? Of course, EJ. He was amazing from the moment he knew. But he was already being super positive and excited, and I didn't want to bum him out or scare him with the truth: that I wasn't okay. In hindsight, maybe he was being that way to encourage me. I guess I was confused by all my conflicting feelings and stifled by not knowing how to sort them out and with whom. I didn't want to dim my husband's or anyone's excitement. This deal was going down, so I assumed I would just get there, get on board, and be thrilled. Misguided assumptions for sure, but I didn't know how to wrap my head around this and get to that joyous, blessing-acceptance stage where I had been before with my other babies. Bottom line: I was having a hard time thinking straight. Or thinking at all. The demands of life became a welcome distraction.

Who Says That?

Have you ever stood outside in the soft, gentle rain with your tongue out, enjoying the cool bath of raindrops—the serene life-supporting rain, the fresh smells, and the gentle rhythmic embrace of it all? I guess I thought that's what it was going to be like sharing our news. People would be surprised, but they'd also be gentle, kind and supportive, celebratory and fun, right?

Turned out, I was looking for the gentle rain, but it was more like getting pelted in a hail storm, sometimes just by small stinging pieces, other times by pieces the size of golf balls, which were painful and left a bruise. I was grateful for the kind and supportive souls, but they were shockingly few and far between. The variety of reactions I experienced came in groups…

The Recycled Plastics

Funny how they came in categories. There were your plastic people: the ones who turn your monosyllabic name into three syllables that cover two octaves as they say it. They'd put on an insincere smile and say, "Lyyy-yyy-nnnnnn! Oh, wow, that's great for you. An 'oops' baby. A mistake. Well that will change things. Hehehe. Good luu-uuck!" Without fail they whispered to their husbands, with no effort to even try to keep it secret, "Honey, you are to get checked first thing tomorrow." Or, "You are not even coming near me until you are checked." Or they would slowly and physically move away from me like I had the power to impregnate them on the spot. Cool super-power to consider, but really?!

The Extremes

The extreme commenters left me scratching my head. For example, one lovely religious lady actually said this to me: "Oh, Lynn… I'm… so, um, yes, happy for you! That's great! Wow, at forty-three… yeah, but if that were me, I'd kill myself!" So, let me get this straight—you would kill yourself and the baby, therefore, that would be two deaths, from your own hand. How does that square? Not being judgmental here, just saying what she was saying, know what I'm saying? You could also say she was "just saying that" or being dramatic. True, but the effect on me was really devastating. My situation was so unacceptable to her that she would, joking or not, off herself. I would love to be able to say I was not affected and just gestated on.

The Shamers

Some seemed to want to simply shame or school me. I would be accosted by women at school who "somehow" found out about my bonus baby. I got this feeling I was all of a sudden Rizzo from the movie *Grease*: "Step aside, lady with a baby." I was the defective typewriter, missing a period.

One gal saw me at the school pickup and came up to me with her take. Because I asked for her opinion. Not. "Ooooh, Lyyyyynn, really? Don't you know BY NOW how these things happen? How things work? Haven't you figured this out? Best to you, of course (of course), but (pause for an emphasized, breathy) wow." She actually left shaking her head. I wonder if she ever considered how lacerated that left me. I was already feeling fragile about all this. And what was I supposed to say? "Oh, um, yep, I've heard of intercourse before. Yep, got a good idea the sperm and the egg bit is the real deal. Noticed that with my three kids before this. Even planned for it. So, I'm not an imbecile, but,…" Maybe I really was contagious? I would have made a dash to the fertility clinic if for a second it would have helped someone with this get-you-pregnant-around-me aura I had.

The Accusers

This next group is "fun". Hold on to your hat, because it's probably what everyone was thinking but... wasn't classless enough to say.

One such encounter happened when we were with a group of people at a gathering, all the kids running around—your typical fun scene. A woman I had just met, offered me a glass of wine. Even though we were just starting to share the information, I looked at EJ, and we smiled at each other like, yep, let's share it! So, I told her I'd pass on the wine, that I was actually expecting. "Oh! Great!" she replied. For some stupid reason we launched into some of the details about this being a bonus baby, and that we had learned a little about how "yeah, things grow back".

This was when the men started patting EJ on the back, the crowd marveling about his manhood and basically lifting him on their shoulders as though he had scored the victorious shot at the buzzer.

This woman was somehow able to screech above the din, which was nice because then all my children could hear her, "Oh my God, you must have had an affair!! I mean that just doesn't happen. I've never heard of that before! You know you only get pregnant one way, and you must have stepped out... that HAD to be it!"

I was in a state of complete and total shock. My mind went straight to stun gun. Off the tip of my tongue, ready to slice and dice, I said, "Okay, you got me. Yep, had an affair and got knocked up. And your husband... well, he was just okay. But he owes me college funding."

Okay, I ALMOST said that. Of course, I looked up and saw my kids, who were trying to make out what weird energy was coming their way from this conversation. Dang high road. Instead, I mumbled that an affair wouldn't occur to me and then made my way to the bathroom feeling neutered and embarrassed for nothing. Well, maybe embarrassed about matching her idiocy with that comeback I almost unleashed and was still wrestling with whether or not I should have said…

Deciding in the bathroom I would not cry at such an unfair assault, I just sat there for a bit. What was going on here? People were saying the craziest things. I needed support and a little kindness. A little help adapting. Not verbal assassination.

Another interesting side effect of this exchange was the explanation that followed when my youngest asked me what the word "affair" meant.

The Random

Announcing a conception usually evokes a manly "attaboy" and a feminine knowing. This sharing was different with all its electrical undercurrents of sideways glances and (not so) hidden "holy craps".

Want some more? Here goes:

"Do you know how old you will be when the baby graduates from high school?" Yep, I can do the math. At least I didn't hear that seventeen times…

"Oh, you will have SO much help from the other kids— it will be just a piece of cake." Really? Do all their needs vanish? I'm sure they'll be thrilled as I'm napping to change diapers, cook, clean, plot, plan, get uniforms, and make sure they weren't missing any key developmental requirements.

"You will be busy, but it will all seem like nothing with that sweet little one in your arms." Great, I'll let you know what my family likes for dinner and when to bring the other three to all their activities. You'll be right, it will seem like nothing. And I won't have to drive impaired from sleep deprivation. Good point!

This one hit a very painful nerve of fear I had been harboring: "I'm sure it will all be okay with having three other "normal" children since the statistics for babies after forty are a little scary for birth defects, I've heard. Best to you!" As if that nagging worry, okay panic, wasn't just below the surface. The only defect I noticed, though, was her thinking it was okay to SAY that to me.

Here's a funny one: One woman came up to me to "congratulate" me on the news after she'd heard that I was expecting. After a cautious thank-you on my part... wait for it... she said, "I heard about it and just had to hear the real story! Because I've already told my husband to RUN to the urologist and get checked. I mean, that would be the worst, right? Faced with another pregnancy right now would be, well, oh, oops, um, it will be great and, um... congrats to you!" It was one of those humorous times when I could tell she was trying to get herself to stop talking but only kept digging deeper. I wanted to just say, "Yeah, it's the worst. Thanks for the reminder."

The High-Pitched Pollyannas

The Pollyanna ones were bust-out funny: "Oh, how wooooonderrrrfulllll! (in a high, squeaky voice). God has blessed you! Your life is so perfect and now a new baaay-beeee! Do you just feel like you are on a cloud!? Gliding along in bliss. Two boys and two girls are just perfect!" Rough decision there—to just slap the snot out of her? Stare blankly and waddle off? Or bust out laughing (and deal with the leakage)? I'm an optimistic person, but please tell me I've never been a smarmy fool, completely unaware of where someone might be at on an emotional level? If so, I'm SORRY! For real, sorry.

The Supportive

Don't get me wrong, there were certainly wonderful moments too. When we told my sister-in-law, Fran, that we were expecting our fourth, she immediately jumped up, ran over to me, and hugged me profusely. She was over-the-moon excited and didn't hesitate to express that. She gushed about a new baby and was so happy to her core. I just wanted to melt. AND, this was from a woman who always wanted to have a baby herself. She and her husband had tried for years to have a baby, and it just didn't happen for her. Fortunately for them, they adopted a beautiful girl, and it completed their family. So, even telling her, I felt very sheepish and inwardly guilty about my selfish reservations. Here's someone who would have given anything. Sadly, Fran would end up not having the chance to even meet the baby.

Another friend found out in a fun, different-than-hoped-for way. My youngest was in kindergarten, and once a week I went to volunteer and teach the class sign language. We were working on the pledge of allegiance for the kindergarten play. When the time was right (baby bump was starting to bump), I had my daughter get up in front of the class with the teacher and my friend, who was the para, in the room.

Or so I thought. My friend had just run out of the room to make copies! So, my daughter signed, "My mom is having a baby." The teacher, who was learning along with the class, slowly digested the signs. The class asked my daughter to repeat it and she did. The teacher then looked at me and said, "Does she have her signs confused or... are you... um... sending me another kindergartner in the future?"

I nodded to the teacher, and she laughed in such a kindly way and gave me a big hug. It was sweet and so appreciated. The kids in the class reacted like five-year-olds: Is it a boy or a girl? What's its name? When can we see it? Too cute. I handed out Baby Ruth candy bars to celebrate (remain calm—this perfect mom knew there were no nut allergies).

So, walking out of the classroom, I saw my friend coming back down the hall. I have no idea how she'd heard already, but she came running to me and asked if it was true that I was having a baby. I said yes, and honestly, braced myself for the usual comments. Nope! She was ecstatic! She literally jumped up and down with joy and was SO excited. I mean, she dropped her copies and jumped up and down, right then and there. She's very athletic, so she was getting up there too. It helped my spirits so much in that moment I wanted to cry and drink in those soft, gentle rain drops of her words and actions.

I made a mental note to myself to be sure I behaved like that no matter the experience a person shared with me: soft, gentle rain to the spirit.

The Painfully Honest

Another friend of mine was pregnant at the same time and due in June, four months before my due date. A few of us were throwing her a baby shower, as we chicks do. I was over at the hostess's house setting up and getting ready. Another soccer mom dropped off both our sons at this same house, helping us out, again as we mom-chicks do for each other. She walked in and saw the decorations and the "Welcome Baby" theme. Unsolicited, she said, "You're having a baby shower? Who's the poor sucker? I mean, really, I couldn't imagine it!" My friend and I just looked at each other, knowingly. I looked at the soccer mom and said, "Well, what could be so bad, right? You have four kids." She said, "Yeah, shoot me now." Avoiding the complications of shooting another human and all the red tape and paperwork that would entail, I just said, "Well, guess what? I'm expecting. Guess that makes me the sucker who can imagine it." I was able to laugh along because she was so busted with the truth. Her truth. After so many comments, this one didn't sting too bad. Perhaps I was getting used to this? Finding acceptance? Well, let's not push it.

In hindsight, I wish I would have just been able to say, "Look, I'm the container in this. The incubator. But other forces are at work here. Beats me what they are. In the meantime, I would appreciate some support, kind words, or, if that's not possible, carry on as I remain calm."

I had to think, was this just going to be my new normal? And when did I choose this freaky victim role? Like so many people with their personal experiences, I continued on with my growing little one in silent disorientation. I was embarrassed to say to anyone that I was sad and struggling and feeling psycho, and in the next breath I was also excited and loving the sweetness growing in my belly. Make up your mind. Or better yet, they might just mumble, "You've got issues."

The Parents

Living far away from my parents, I had to tell them over

the phone. I felt bummed out by that because we told them with no fanfare that I was pregnant and that it looked like the baby was due in early October. There was total silence. Pin-drop silence (yep, another pregnant pause). "Are you still there? Hello?" Then my mom started laughing—haha funny—not gonna fall for that! EJ had a history of messing with them before and in between each of our other three being born. I could understand her disbelieving response. Dad was still silent.

So, I went down the road of convincing them that it was the real deal. I could send a picture of the two blue lines if needed. Or the ultrasound photos. We kept talking and shared that "things grow back" and that we were now expecting our fourth! Yay! They were still silent. "Hello?" (I knew this should have been in person.)

Dad piped in after several minutes (seriously, several minutes), "That is great! Now you'll have four kids like we did—haha. Congratulations! And we get to add to the grandkid total." After rambling on a bit more (can't even remember what I said, probably stuff about the surgery and having a C-section), my mom finally came up for air. She said she believed me. This was at least ten minutes later. I thought I would fall off my chair! She'd been thinking this was a prank the whole time and didn't want to fall for it. Can't blame her, I guess—I had been thinking the same way too. She was finally able to wrap her head around the reality of my having a baby "older" and said, "Well, if any two people should have more kids in this world, and can handle this beautifully, it would be you two."

As the tears fell down my face, I thanked them for their support and told them I would let them know as things moved along. Why is it your parents have a path straight to your heart when you need acceptance and true support?

What I didn't realize until much later, my mom's extended silence was also due to her worry about the toll it would take on me and the complications. Moms, such worriers.

The Other "Grandmotherly Support"

Being involved in a book club was awesome for me. I love reading books and discussing them and seeing other points of view. I'd been in this book club for at least six years at the time. It was very special to me and perfect because all the other ladies (five of them) were older than me by at least fifteen years, which made the points of view even more special/impactful for me. They were at a different point in life. I loved their life-stage perspective on things when we were reviewing books. We intentionally kept it a small group, with up to six at any one time. I knew my sweet group would have to be included in my pregnancy in a fun way. They may not have been ready for this name, but in my head, I was thinking of them as my "granny group".

We met at the house of one of our members. She had a lovely lunch for us, and it was a nice spring day. Flowers had started to bloom, giving everything a very fertile feel. At the end of the book discussion, I had a little goodie bag for each member with a Baby Ruth candy bar (I guess that had become my little gimmick), and I think a little pink something. I handed them out and said I had news, guess what? They opened their goodies and came up with some random guesses, all wrong! Gosh, I'd thought it was obvious, but I would have to hint on. I started to say something about the name Ruth, was going to say that every baby is not named Ruth, when the hostess's husband came in. His wife said to him, "Look, Lynn just gave us this candy and—"

He interrupted, "Oh, congrats on having a baby!"

The ladies were like, wait, what? When they all looked at me, I said, "Bingo". They were shocked, excited, and amazed this dude got it before they did! Of course, I had to launch into the failed vasectomy details, five-and-a-half-years, and that I, myself, still remained in shock.

What a delicious and merciful relief it was for me not to have to field crazy questions or deal with off-based judgments, thoughtlessness, and ridiculous comments. Pure support. Pure excitement and plans to fight over holding the baby during future book clubs. I was grateful to tears.

The Men

Strangely, or not so strangely, the reaction from men and our men friends was somewhat annoying. To me. Irritatingly, most of the men carried on about my husband's total manliness. "Can't keep a good man down." Absolutely. Right. For sure. He deserves that. But what about after the nine minutes? What about the nine months carrying a baby? At 'advanced maternal age'? Instead, EJ became the cat's meow.

Most men still recoiled in fear, along with their wives, at the thought of a surprise baby, but not at the same level as their wives. We all imagine our own role if this were to happen to us, therefore, the women were clearly more freaked out. The men don't carry the little bundle or have their body misshapen and have to face labor, but instead, they have a whole set of different fears.

A lot of them seemed to love the math problems, calculating EJ's age at various milestones. Several talked about whether EJ would even know if the nest had emptied or would he be too senile? How old would he be when she graduated high school or college? Would he even be there when she graduated college? Would he know it? But the biggest was the Tarzan chest pounding that always came back to his potency. His favorite saying was "can't keep a good man down," but many more were added:

- The Spermanator
- Go Swim Team!
- Vas of Steel
- Evil Knievel sperm
- Me and Chuck Norris: Vasectomies fear us.

There was certainly celebration around his sperm. Not once did anyone marvel at my fertility—my body's amazing ability to implant a fertilized egg even through a surgery "down there". Or its ability to keep the pregnancy at this age. No amazement to see this thing through with all the physical requirements. No appreciation for the change in life for me or my next steps. Nary a thought of that. Why not a little…

- Fertile and Over 40 Rockstar
- Conceiver Receiver
- Wonder Womb-an
- Incredible Incubator
- 40+ and Fertile
- Power Baby Maker
- Mature and Mating
- Experienced Reproducer
- Pro-Procreator
- Serial Conceiver
- Knocked Up but Not Out
- Immaculate Conceiver
- Implantress… (my favorite)

Y'know, just sayin'.

At least I never heard any of the men encourage EJ to look at me funny or demand a paternity test. That I know of. Hmmmm. Naw, better off not knowing if anyone went down that path with him. Come to think of it, EJ wouldn't have allowed that conversation to get off the ground to any level if some "friend" thought to question. He was better than I was at dealing with crappy comments. Growing up with ten brothers and sisters probably helped with that. His hormones may have been a bit more even as well.

6

What Once Seemed So Important...

I am not a violent person. It usually takes me a bit to even get mad. But honestly, if I had to hear "advanced maternal age" one more time during this process, someone was gonna get slapped. It sounded to me more like "ancient mama" or "knocked-up grandma". Forty-three and pregnant: someone get a wheelchair, stat. Once, while a nurse reviewed my chart she looked up like, "Wow, how is it possible this human is alive? I've heard of these things in the *Enquirer*, but right here in front of me?!" Okay, I may exaggerate some, but it is incredible how the medical community has its labels and its reactions and its methodologies that stick to the script only. When you are going through prenatal care, you are seen by plenty of providers along the way. Which is great. But each one feels free to pile on their comments too. Well, heck, the target or "kick me" sign was already fastened on my back, right? Or at least in my chart. I don't think they realize their cumulative effect either. You go in and get weighed, various vitals are taken, and a discussion on any developments ensues. On one of my visits this individual commented (for real), "Oh, I see you are of advanced maternal age. A geriatric pregnancy. Interesting," and made a note in my chart. I was thinking, what? What's wrong? What did you just write? What's interesting? Why?

Then the doctor would come in, do the exam, and speak to me with comments like, "Given the circumstances… " and "Because of the situation, we need to be cautious here or pay attention to… ". It all felt so worrisome. Then at checkout, the lady behind the desk would kindly ask, how is everything going? I would think, oh, great, now she is going to give me that knowing, pitying head nod. A patronizing, "It will all be okay." How would she know? What's okay anyway? Yeah, maybe I was just slightly sensitive.

Off to see the ultrasound team. I checked in and the gal mentioned again, "Oh, advanced maternal age, I see. Good to know. Hmmm. Please have a seat and they'll be right with you." Then a bit louder, "PLEASE HAVE A SEAT, THEY WILL BE RIGHT WITH YOU." Or was that my imagination? I looked at EJ, and he seemed not to notice. We waited in the waiting room, with its newly renovated look of creams, browns, and yellows. Thank goodness the pastel ducks and little zoo animals were not the scenery. I couldn't handle that. Like back when maternity outfits used to be so virginal looking. Who are you kidding? I looked around and checked out the magazines, which were there for my entertainment so I wouldn't notice how long I'd had to wait. I swore I caught the receptionist checking me out. EJ noticed it as well and we just smiled—the look of been here, done that, have the stretch marks.

We were invited to follow the hostess of this party down the hall to our sweet little ultrasound suite. I was given the instructions to slap on the gown and please get on the table. I could set my walker in the corner out of the way. I did as I was told, and EJ and I got excited about finding out the gender. We hadn't done that with the other three. I always felt after the hard work of labor, it was nice to have that fun surprise at the end of the effort. In this case, the surprise was already front and center, so preparing with pinks or blues seemed like a better idea than waiting, especially since most everything baby—pink, blue, or otherwise—had been given away or sold or had broken down.

The ultrasound technician came in looking at the chart, said a pleasant hello while still reading, and then looked up. "Oh, hi. So, we have an advanced maternal age situation here. Okay, good to know." (Again, why?) I asked if that impacted this procedure, and the answer was, well, um, no. I didn't fully realize in the moment that it meant they were more tuned into looking for potential problems, signs of birth defects, and such.

As the tech started to put the goopy goo on my belly which is used to create a good connection and good read on the ultrasound, I braced myself. Apparently in the last seven years since I had experienced this process, somebody got the memo that the goopy goo was COLD! This time it was delightfully warmed in some sort of warmer container before it was applied. Nice. I even said out loud, "Wow, that is pleasantly warm. Is that a new feature to the procedure?" "Yep, we realized how uncomfortable the cold stuff was and now have it in a warmer," I was told. How downright civilized.

This moment for expecting couples is one of the best.

Getting to see the child growing inside you, moving around and all its parts, is nothing less than breathtaking. Everything else seems to melt away. And for the father, it must be mesmerizing to see everything happening in real time, that he otherwise takes on faith. For him (and me) to see the hands move or the baby sucking its thumb is mind-blowing. We just enjoyed the moment of feeling so bonded and connected to each other. They asked if we wanted to know the gender… Of course! You are having a… baby girl. "What?!" We said at the same time, "Perfect!" That makes two of each.

By then another tech had joined in and said, "Oh, this is your fourth?" Yes, a beautiful bonus baby. Bonus baby? And, well, we launched into the story a little bit. I still felt kind of cautious or exposed from all the reactions I'd experienced at that point (and I was in the little thin gown deal). But, I also thought this would be a good time to ask her if she had seen this before. If anyone had known about "vasectomy grow-backs" it would be them, right? So, I asked if they had seen this before and how often. They mused a little bit back and forth and said they had seen, usually, pregnancy after tubal ligation. Interesting (my turn). They remembered a colleague in the last twelve months who had seen a vasectomy baby. I thought, I should find out who those people were and chat with them. How were they doing? How did they manage through the shock? I started to wonder how many people experienced this type of thing, from "recanalization" (failed vasectomy), or a tubal ligation that regenerated, or other miraculous conceptions. Did they live to tell? Did these other prolific parents have any advice? Were they ancient too? Comforting words? Secret sauce? Wait, pass on the sauce.

Turns out less than one percent of vasectomies grow

back. One study (US Collaborative Review of Sterilization [CREST]) followed 540 couples and found six women to become pregnant, three of those in the first three months. Two of the women reported their partner didn't follow the follow-up. Researchers estimate that 1 in 100 vasectomies fails within five years, with user error (not getting checked up and verifying there are no swimmers) seemingly being the major cause. It makes our little sweetheart even more meant to be miraculous. There was follow-up. There were checks. Verifications. Guarantees. Okay, maybe not so much on the guaranteed part. I think we may have even signed something about that.

Unfortunately, the most concerning outcome of the ultrasound was that they urged me to have an amniocentesis. Apparently, they saw some thicker skin around the back of the neck and other unspecified reasons to indicate a need for an amnio. Also, shocker, because of my "advanced maternal age" it was already highly recommended. Thankfully, because of my advanced maternal maturity, I was a little more ready to question it and not just blindly say okay. I asked why. They very gingerly said "just to be sure"—to check for Down's and other possibilities. It would give me information to make any decisions. Oh, got it.

Since I wasn't planning to terminate even if the child had a special need, I wondered why it was necessary, especially with the risks. They really were strongly encouraging me to do the amnio, and when I thought about it, it could be helpful to know ahead, so I decided to do it. I could get in support groups and get counseled on what to expect and how to manage and take care of this baby if it had additional support needs.

Amnio Angst

I was pretty nervous the day of the procedure. The looming risks, of course, were the possibility of puncture damage, which can cause the loss of the baby. EJ was there with me, always a huge comfort. He had his own nervousness too. I also wasn't sure how painful it would be. You hear all sorts of stories. It added extra fun to the party that I was required to have a full bladder. Did I mention my three previous children, one at ten pounds-ish? A full bladder at this point brought its own particular agony. Again, I suited up with the gown (probably should have started a collection of those along the way). I was brought into the "operating room," which really was how it felt: dark and cold, very dim lights. Center stage was the table with a huge light over it. I got on the table and settled in. I wondered, maybe we could start this deal with a glass of red wine?

The specific doctor for this procedure came in and greeted us. "Hello, Mrs. Bodnar. Oh, I see, advanced maternal age." I wanted to go all instantaneous musical on him— break out in song and dance. Can you see it? Jumping off the table, the music starts, and we sing out the wonderful news of the day: Advanced Maternal Age! We have backup singers and dancers and pull off a whole peachy number while the doctor and nurse have stage faces of surprise and awe. With overly large gestures they check the chart. On the very last note, timed perfectly, I land back on the table, hubby next to me in his place, and the baby places a perfectly timed kick for an exclamation point. Okay, let's just say my imagination can get out there sometimes, and why not get creative rather than crabby for the 100th proclamation of "advanced maternal age"? I laughed to myself thinking of it, though. Instead, it was a mumbled, yes, advanced maternal age... so I've been told.

Instead of a perky musical, it was more like listening to golf announcers. Which I never really understood—they have their whispery hushed voices describing the golfers and their shots, but are the announcers really right there? At each hole? Or watching in the clubhouse where they could yell and the golfer wouldn't ever hear them?

Okay, sorry, I digress. The doctor and nurses asked me in their perfect NPR tone to lie back and try to relax. They plainly and calmly talked me through each step. Was I ready? "Yes," I said. In my head I wasn't so sure. I gave EJ a look that only he would know was my "scared but I can do this" look. He gave me his look that only I would know was his "this will be okay, and we are here together."

At first, they walked me through the steps, but then they got pretty quiet. I think the ginormous needle they poke into your gut even intimidates them. So, they may not want to slip and say, "Wow! It worked again to get this three-foot needle into the exact place we hoped it would land!" By then with the pain and screaming bladder, I was rockin' some low-level labor breathing so I may not have heard them walk through anything.

It seemed like it took a long time and then not so long either. You know what I mean? Pretty soon they were saying I could get up and get dressed. I asked if they saw anything or could make any observations. No. Just no. I would have to talk to my doctor. He would be getting ahold of me within about forty-eight hours. This was a Monday.

As we checked out, I confirmed that we would hear something in a day or two. The nurse said yes, of course, Wednesday or early Thursday at the very latest. I could feel the stress and angst of waiting, wondering, fearing, and hoping set in. Just think positive. Two impossible blue lines worth of positive.

I would just distract myself. Surely tons of pending moms have to wait for these results all the time. Tons of people everywhere were waiting for results that week, I was sure. For all sorts of things. Great news. The most feared news. What we all had in common was the agonizing waiting. Just think about that, Lynn, I would tell myself. It wouldn't change the truth, it would just be revealed or shared. There were worse things to wait for. Right. Okay, so, that didn't work. Nice try. It occupied all my brain space trying to preoccupy myself.

Tuesday, I spent doing my usual running, kid prep, meals, chores. It was early May, and there were lots of end-of-year school stuff to contend with. District track meet, soccer tourneys, teacher appreciation, field trips, permission forms, and on and on. I was just taking on all those details and trying to move along under the overcast cloud of worry. At the end of the day, I put my head on the pillow, grateful I was one day closer to having the results and "knowing" my next steps of what to prepare for. I guess I had to come to terms with how anxious and worried I was while trying to avoid another (or a continuing) reaction of "ungraceful" denial, this time of a potential special needs baby. I believed I would be expected to have a certain happy/accepting reaction and would need to endure the next level of criticism and brutal comments concerning a baby with special needs, and how my age or mistakes were to blame or whatever. I thought I should have this gracious response ready and been so accepting of the possibility in retrospect. Say to who?

Wednesday—a new day! Good morning! Today was the day I would hear from the doctor. Yep, "get it done!"

Nothing all morning. Tick. Tock. So, I rid myself of all my "normal" stuff to do and worked on organizational projects. I started thinking about a wall that needed a pictorial family history map. This was clearly a nesting instinct and perhaps self-survival in engaging my mind elsewhere until the call. Just before going to get the kids that afternoon, I had my friend call me to be sure my phone was working. Not the normal thing to do, but what if, right? Phone worked. Still nothing.

Thursday. Okay, they said by yesterday, so today was a sure thing. Thank goodness because my worry and stress were probably causing other problems with the baby. As much as I tried, I just couldn't chill, and it was causing significant stress. EJ had his hands full just trying to get me to not worry, to talk about other stuff. Again, 3:30 p.m. rolled around. I needed to pick up the kids. Answering that type of call in front of them was not optimal. So, prior to pick up, I called the doctor's office, asking if the results were in and could I find out what they are? "I'll check and get back to you. If not by the end of today, tomorrow for sure." Nice. You do that. Go home, enjoy your world. I'll be here by the phone waiting for my sanity to make an appearance. Have a nice evening.

No. Call.

Friday noon was happening, and my phone was not ringing. I decided to walk the dog the very long way around my neighborhood to calm down. Instead, I got home and felt more exhausted, and I clearly "knew" it could only be bad news because they hadn't called yet. The doctor himself must make the call for the bad news, and he's probably been busy. That's the only explanation. Okay, start to think about that and accept the fact that your bonus baby was now going to have special needs that you had no clue how to take care of. We would adapt. Lots of people have figured this out. I would get help and do what needed to be done. We would pull together as a family and rally. We would have more compassion and understanding, right?! And then… the phone rang.

In a single bound I dove like a parkour expert and said hello before my heart could manage another beat. Only to find out it was some rando who wanted to know if I wanted to donate something to someone. I absentmindedly agreed to hand over my kidney at a future date to someone, somewhere. It was infuriatingly NOT the doctor.

As I saw the clock ticking toward the school pickup time AND the end of the workweek (can you imagine two MORE days of this?), I called the doctor again. My special friend with her weekend plans already set, picked up. Um, yes, I called yesterday to get the results of my amnio that were due Thursday at the latest. I'm quite anxious. Can you please, possibly, find out the status of things for me before the weekend? I have been waiting since Monday and have a lot of angst as more time goes on. Can you help? Yes, of course. Hold, please. Three minutes of scratchy music later, she got back on and said the doctor would be contacting me with these results, but it seemed he may have left for the weekend. Boom! I exploded! No, not a temper-fueled rant. Just spontaneous combustion. I was now going to be in the fetal position all weekend (pardon the pun).

So, Jack and I would be hanging out. Jack Daniels. Actually not—do you really think I'd risk that after worrying so much about the amnio!? No, the doctor did not call on Friday. Or Saturday. Or Sunday. And the fact that the doctor had to call me and talk to me made it worse. There is only one reason why only the doctor can talk to you to share results: it's bad news. But not officially, because I didn't actually talk to him and know for sure. Every ounce of my being would be dedicated to grasping on to my remaining sliver of hope. My self-talk was like a ventriloquists' convention for the imbalanced.

After a weekend of living on autopilot, like making food for my family and wondering how it got there, Monday finally arrived. By 6 a.m., no one had called yet. I got everyone off to school and then I wondered if I should just drive to the doctor's office and wait, staring through his office window like a stalker until he talked to me. At 9 a.m. on the dot—the second they will answer the phones—I called and asked all the, now usual, questions. I was told to be patient (I really did want to scream, "Screw you! You be patient!") and that he would call me today.

I sat by the phone and held my breath. Just kidding. I waited, again trying to distract myself with just about anything. After lunch, about 1 p.m.-ish, I decided to walk the dog. Sweet awesome Wrigley and I would chase some bunnies, sniff some stuff, and hang out. Of course, my cell phone was already crazy glued to my hand for sure-thing answering. Well into our walk, as we were on the sidewalk circling one of the lakes in the hood, my phone rang. It was the doctor's office. I answered and told them to please hold. Okay, just kidding. It was a female's voice saying she wanted to discuss my amnio results.

All I could detect was that it was a female's voice. Not the doctor's, a male. The doctor was the one who gives the bad news! I was able to discern her saying that there were no defects detected, no Down's, no spina bifida, and so forth.

I dropped directly to my knees, I would love to say

intentionally thanking God, but honestly my legs just gave out. I had myself so worked up and worried and overburdened with the "How will I… " that the moment of "It's okay" overwhelmed me.

At one point I heard, "Mrs. Bodnar, are you there?"

Um, yes, thank you for the call and the results. I was too grateful to provide constructive feedback on the torture of waiting a week for life-changing news that was promised in forty-eight hours.

Looking at it later, it was totally and completely all about expectations. If they had said it would be one to two weeks, it would have been different, right? Right. Okay, kind of.

Just wait until I get ahold of their "How are we doing?" survey. I'll make them wait a week or so for those results… And, I get it, they probably don't even read them.

I felt like I was spiraling down, accelerated by this agonizing amnio experience. On the edge silently screaming, but no one could hear because it wasn't allowed. No screaming, no complaining. Smile and nod with gracious acceptance and simply dust off unpleasant comments. If the unspoken feelings were not allowed, then do they really happen? If a tree falls in the woods…? (Were there other moms silently struggling all around me about lots of issues in their worlds?)

And then, suddenly, life happens and hands you something that makes all these things seem so relatively small. The tree does fall in the woods, you do hear it, and it hits everyone, hard.

Tragedy Strikes

Even though I had often felt like my life was one big squirrel-fest, and that my ability to concentrate was pushed out when my first baby was pushed out, tragedies have a way of slowing down time and making you really see that living in each moment isn't a pithy saying, it's vital.

In a typical flurry of activity, driving with the noise level reaching rock concert decibels in my car (like texting is the only distraction to drivers... don't tell lawmakers, they could outlaw kids in cars), I pulled in to pick up my oldest from soccer practice. The other two kids were in the car doing something loudly, and I was working my belly out around the steering wheel. I was turning the corner on being six months along with the bonus baby.

My phone rang, which it usually does when your hands are full and your timing is the tightest. I managed to answer but dropped it on the car floor, under the steering wheel. I had to angle it just right to grab the phone, squeezing between the wheel and my belly, while trying to still breathe. Finally hearing who it was, a family friend said, "Lynn, I need to tell you something." I started saying that I had accidentally dropped my phone and blathered on, "Oh, sorry, just the usual spaz here. What's up?"

He said, "Lynn, stop, this is serious."

The tone of his voice yanked me present, and with immediate clarity, I was in a dead stop, all chaos around me was instantly shut out.

My sister-in-law had been in an accident. She was horseback riding with her friend when her dog went into an irrigation ditch. Since it was late May in Colorado, the mountain water runoff was flowing strongly and rapidly. Fran (EJ's sister that I've known since I was about fifteen years old) got off her horse and got a big stick to try to get the dog to bite onto it so she could help haul her out. Unfortunately, she was wearing her cowboy boots, which caused her to slip into the ditch as well.

Her friend, at first, didn't think it was a problem, because

Fran stood up and seemed like she had her footing and would make it to the bank of the ditch. But suddenly, she slipped and went under the strong current, and her friend couldn't see her at all, only later to find out she had sustained a serious head injury and was swept downstream. She was recovered by emergency responders and transported to the hospital, in critical condition.

All time seemed to stop. I got the kids home from soccer practice as soon as possible and got to my husband. He hadn't heard the news about his sister yet. I was sitting in his office with a drained, faraway scared look for the second time in a matter of months. I shared the details that I knew in the most clear, gentle, and concise way possible so we could both grasp the situation at hand. I don't even remember who I called last minute to help me with the kids that night, but it allowed us to rush over to the hospital. My heart broke as the gravity of the situation became agonizingly clear.

Family members were notified and naturally came to town in large numbers (did I mention he had ten siblings?). Suddenly, my house was a buzzing bed and breakfast. Which, of course, was fine. I did the best I could to help accommodate. Fran's husband kept everyone involved and graciously supported her family in so many ways. Even in his time of confusion, grief, disbelief—shock, denial, and pain, fearing the worst. Breaking our hearts, she passed on June 1st. She left behind her husband and her daughter, eighteen years old at the time. She left me with so many wonderful memories, not the least of which was her beautiful, supportive, loving reaction to me and my bonus baby.

What I noticed was Fran's husband kept saying things out loud that needed to be done—for the wake, for the funeral. He was just saying them, but no one was writing them down or saying, "I'll do that." What got me was how he mentioned that he had to get this whole thing right because she would have eternity to "discuss" it with him if he messed up. Funny, but there was also meaning there, the hope of an eternal relationship and being together again. My heavy heart was deeply touched.

I started writing down what he wanted done. I worked with the funeral director and made action-item lists, assigning people to each item. I coordinated with my brother-in-law and the priest to discuss the funeral service. I took notes on what they talked about to communicate with the funeral director, making sure he was on top of all the details that were important.

Fran was a beautiful singer and once performed "Ave Maria" at the Vatican. This was recorded at the time, and it was decided that it would be included in the funeral. It was incredibly beautiful and equally painful now that she was gone. A beautiful mother singing about a beautiful mother. I was lucky to know ahead of time that this video would be included because I would have totally started sobbing—the real, ugly, snotty kind—and would have not been able to stop. With pregnancy hormones and my natural inclination to cry at Hallmark commercials, I wouldn't have had a chance. And there was work to be done.

We lined up the meals, pallbearers, songs, readings, and all. There were so many details. Even though her husband was holding up amazingly, he wasn't in the frame of mind to make those details happen. And Fran was the mom, so she usually did all the details anyway. I supported him by helping to pick out the casket. We worked with the funeral home on how the wake would go, the hours, and that we could bring food in for the visitation. My wonderful village of friends asked what they could do to help. They kindly brought snacks, nibbles, and sweets for everyone at the wake. Coincidentally (or not), it was the same people, just like Fran, who were over the moon about my bonus baby, who brought food and support.

After the final ceremony and lowering of the casket, my mama bear hormones were on high alert as someone said to my niece, who had just buried her mother, "Oh my gosh, you are SO skinny. Too skinny! You really need to eat something! If you came to my house, I would get you some food and fatten you up!"

Once again, a "lovely" self-focused, think-they-are-funny person absolutely destroying another with their intrusive, clueless comments. She came over to me, tears upon tears, and told me what had just happened. Something just snapped in me, and I was ready to kick some serious ass. The hurtful comments I was regularly experiencing were one thing, but to this devastated girl who JUST BURIED HER MOTHER?!? Can you not contain your comments and just give a hug or kind word? Do you need to judge and condemn? I'm begging for the slightest bit of empathy or self-control. Maybe sometimes people with this tendency need to consider that what they think or have to say just isn't that important.

Yep, breathe it in.

I demanded she show me who this imbecile was so I could promptly rip them apart and make a terrible scene that would not soon be forgotten. Fortunately for us all (mostly me, no doubt), she didn't see where she'd walked off to, so I stayed focused on comforting her and encouraging her to let those comments and the hurt float away. Listening to the clueless is like having tea without a teabag. Why drink it in? They're not capable of understanding, so do not take in their words.

Regaining my composure (thanks, honey), we said the final goodbyes and thank-you's and thanked the funeral director for a great job. He asked me to step aside for a moment. Of course, what's up? He then went on to offer me a job for being the coordinator of all the things I had just done for my brother-in-law in the last week. I was so honored when he told me how impressed he was with all the things I had handled and how I had handled them. He said he almost felt like he should already have paid me. Gotta say, it felt great. Outside validation! It was a labor of love to honor my sister-in-law and support my brother-in-law and niece. Something anyone would have done, right? Not the amazing way YOU did, he said. I thanked him and mentioned (as if he couldn't see my rounding, protrusive, advanced maternal age bump) that I would be focused on another labor of love in less than four months.

As I shared with my husband the job offer, and how complimented I felt, he said he wasn't surprised. I have so many amazing, phenomenal qualities that every organization seeks. He's known me a long time and says sweet things like that. Further, he said he literally couldn't afford all that I do and the excellence with which I do things. Of course, to even consider that job is crazy with the new baby and the total needs of running the homestead. Honestly, how much would that add to the kitty? And how much time would I spend on it, including the odd hours it could involve?

I began to wonder, "Why is the stupid W2 so important?" Why would that bring me the gravitas or stamp of approval that I apparently was looking for? Or simply, if someone gave me money for what fills my day, would that create validity?

Hmm, maybe I'll start charging my husband, my kids, the schools, everywhere I volunteer. I could set out a tip jar! I would have "approval" from others and avoid the unpleasant judgmental comments (or would they just switch to my work being lame?). But wait, what did I tell my niece?

The clueless are not capable of understanding—like having tea without a teabag, why drink it in?

The Final ~~Denial~~ Countdown

Seriously, is this happening? Can I press pause?

The long, hot days of late summer kicked in and so did the soccer game going on in my belly as the sweet girl continued to grow and become more active. It was 2007, and the intro of this new gadget, the Apple iPhone, looked like it was just as hot. I was thinking at the time that if it came with a personal cooling fan, it would be the perfect device, but maybe it would still catch on.

I was trying to keep up with normal life, but I had to admit, dang it, that advanced maternal age was a factor in my energy. And mobility. A six, eight, and twelve-year-old keep up a steady pace, and I was trying to keep up too, fooling myself into believing it was possible. My belly and the steering wheel were constantly duking it out. I was trying to keep up with friends, too, who were long past the memory of aching feet, aching back, and the slower rotund waddle. We planned family gatherings that would have previously been a blast and lasted long into the wee hours. Unfortunately, I found myself looking at the clock at 10 p.m. feeling like it was the wee hours. I no longer cleaned up the night of— it just waited for me until the morning. These "normal" barbecues just didn't seem to be as fun.

Summers are normally hot but being pregnant had to add at least ten to twenty degrees to any hot summer day. I was ready to go the way of the loin-cloth if, at any point, it became socially acceptable. What also continued to heat up was my fear. I didn't really know why. It was just a deep-down nagging. I started to see that these fears were NOT entirely about the impending, beautiful bundle of joy. Maybe it had to do with the fact that I was going after the world record for pounding guilt because I didn't have all these beautiful, wispy, glowing mom-to-be expectations. I was panicked. Why? Ah, just stuff it down, I thought. It will just go away. Everything is "fine".

It was an ever-present feeling of instability, like when you spin around on a baseball bat and then try to walk straight. I was trying to come to terms with this huge shift in my life— my expectations, my fears, my isolation, and what was in store for my body. What this meant for my other three and my spouse. What else would this change? I wracked my brain trying to figure out how to get this under my control… and seriously, my guilt was off the charts. This fourth baby was real, and this was happening. Why couldn't I just joyously accept it and be blessed? Really—how many women were going through hellish hormone treatments and years of dashed hopes to conceive a baby? And here's me being ungrateful, selfishly worrying about what could happen with my body and my goals put on hold, having nagging thoughts about being isolated and stuck with the label of the "do-nothing" stay-at-home mom for more years to come. That W2 that I believed would make me respectable would have to wait. With the pounding question: How could I not give my all to this little one like the rest have had?

But, my inner voice would nag, what about me? My time? Wait, Lynn, that's selfish thinking again. If you are going to have a baby it deserves the full you. Psycho much? If I tried to restart a career now, and failed to manage the balance of it well, and she didn't turn out perfect, there would be a clear path back to me putting myself first, and blame would point all its ugly arrows in my direction. "It's the only difference compared to the other three kids," they'd say. I was being so hard on myself and letting it all get the best of me.

But reality is always individualized. It starts with me, filtered by me: my personal beliefs, experiences, perspectives, thoughts, moods, and the MEANING I give to all these thoughts. I respond with my emotions accordingly oriented by my personal awareness. So, the guilt, sadness, loss, and isolation were the unexamined place I was at. With the bombardment of others' comments and evaluations offered up unfiltered and unsolicited, it escalated my state— what I thought was my reality. And I didn't know where to go with that.

Still Trying to Act Normal

It was mid-August and the due date was within six weeks, give or take. We, being from Chicago, had always been Cubs fans. Ask our dog Wrigley (may she rest in peace, but ask our new puppy, Rizzo). We got the disease young and it stuck. Truly not in an obnoxious way (yes, we've seen that), we just love our team, win or lose, and you know the historical record there. So, now we make sure we are at the game in Denver when they are playing the Rockies—our second favorite team.

Being seriously sumo was not going to stop me from being at the Cubbies game. Besides, it was only like a hundred degrees, piece of cake. A large group of us rode down in the comfortable air conditioning and arrived at the car park. Everyone piled out and started the trek to the stadium. Me too. I shortly found out that the harder I tried to fast-waddle, the hotter and harder actual movement became. My pregnancies had never really stopped me before, as I was very active throughout, so I simply expected the same. Advanced maternal age crept in again. Ugh. I was slowing down, getting farther and farther behind everyone else, sweating profusely and trying to breathe.

EJ was there with me and waved the others on. "We'll meet you at the seats," he said, totally cluing in to my state. I felt stupid, frustrated, pissed, and like, "What the heck?" (And most importantly, I couldn't miss the first pitch!) He looked pretty concerned about my overheating. We just took it slow, and I convinced myself I was fine, but honestly my ego was seared. Everyone else would be moving on while I just took care of the basics. Like breathing.

The thought of not being able to keep up got stuck in my head. I just wouldn't accept this reality or the limited options surrounding it. Feeling sorry for myself was an easy out. I didn't want to be boxed in or limited with restricted choices. Left out or left behind, tied down and missing out on what everyone else was doing. When we finally got to the seats and sat down, our friend kindly offered me some Red Hots. The Cubs lost that day but split the series with the Rockies 2–2, in case you were wondering.

Clearly, I was fighting for things to be "normal" and

resisting the change that sat right in my lap. But what was this normal I was fighting for? I started noticing the fog again, the fog I'd been plagued with for years, and it had to do with how I thought I didn't measure up. Like not "using" my education (what does that mean, anyway?). Ambitionless at home, doing... ? Adding to the emptiness was the recognition of the surprising judgment and nasty comparisons by my equally overstretched, fellow moms was more of the norm than I realized. All those moments when others might have pointed out that my kids were not conforming in some way meant something was wrong with me. It seemed harder and harder to let my kids benefit from natural consequences, so that I could save face. And I took this on as if it were normal and believed it was my fault. I wasn't a good enough mom, not very on top of it. That had to be it.

Sticking with Some Traditions

Every July I make a date with each of my children for our back-to-school effort. We plan a whole day: we shop for clothes and school supplies, and they get to pick wherever they want to go for lunch. We set goals and talk about what's up for them. No interruptions—only them for the whole day. I'm not a huge fan of shopping, but I always enjoy these days with each of them and feel like it's a great bonding tradition. The boys are pretty efficient with the shopping part, since they have a list and get to it. It's about what fits and what's not dorky. Each year becomes more efficient because you really can't spend a whole day at Nike. It's simplified down to what they have in stock and if it's in their size. My boys don't usually wear jeans, so most clothes and shoes are in one spot (that's right, Nike, we just do it, and pretty quick). Then we get the school supplies and a big lunch.

My daughter and I also had always enjoyed "our" day, and there were usually many more stops. More time was allowed to goof around while shopping and analyzing what was cute. That was really the only question. We got back by dinner time, and the rest of the family would ask where we went and, of course, where she picked to have our special lunch.

Tired but happy, I was always grateful for the one-on-one time and connection with each of them with this annual tradition.. Plus—DONE! Ready for school, backpacks set, and no running with the last-minute crazed crowd for that exact plastic folder with three punch holes, two pockets, a partridge in a pear tree, in teal with purple trim.

That summer, being "great with child" naturally changed the pace of the day with each of them. The first back-to-school day was with one of the boys. We had our list, the day was planned, and I was hoping for some dining at a large all-you-can-eat buffet. He opted for the local breakfast place. Still perfect. I could order two meals and say he's a growing boy, right? We started strong: had the plan, lists, coupons, and hunger. We set goals during the meal (he wanted to start with the food—love that kid!) and talked about life. I made sure to touch on whether there was anything he wanted to talk about with the baby coming on board in a few short weeks. "Not really", was the response, but I talked a little about breastfeeding, how I would be down for the count after having the baby surgically removed (I was still trying to wrap my head around that too).

I reinforced that he would carry on his normal school, soccer, home life, but it would mean having a little sister hanging around mostly needing my attention. I loved the way he said he was excited for her to come and realized that things would probably change some. We finished up our meal and started in on the clothes and school supplies list—about four stores and then home. And I was completely exhausted. With my infinite denial and frustration, I didn't want to accept that our "easy" normal day had wiped me out.

The next back-to-school date was with my daughter. I went to bed early the night before, ate healthy, fueled up, and did some pregame warmups to get ready. I was determined to be fully there for her; this was not going to slow me down! Her strategy was to get some shopping done first, then eat, then shop some more, and probably stop for dinner, too. Oh boy. Let's do this!! Fist raised, I ran out of the house. I may have, out of the corner of my eye, caught my husband shaking his head, hoping I wouldn't overdo it.

True to form, she shopped 'til I dropped. It was awesome. She tried on a ton of outfits, and I got to see them all. We outright laughed at some—you know, looks cute on the hanger and then… yuck. Or, cute, but could this be any itchier?

I had this strong desire to make sure she knew I was all in with her because the next several months (years) were going to bring so much change. She couldn't possibly understand it, but I wanted her to know I was there for her and always would be. It would just look a bit different for a while. Maybe I was desperately clinging to making this day awesome so I could point back to it when I became far less available to her.

At one point, she asked me if I was okay. I looked really tired, hot and sweaty and was getting slower, she commented. "It's okay if we have to go home," she said. No freaking way. I powered through feeling tired and inadequate, bummed that she had even noticed.

Suddenly, I spotted something I'd never really seen before. You know those "dude" chairs stores have outside fitting rooms for guys to sit in so they won't make their wives bail and they will stay to spend more money? Yeah, baby. I took out a few dudes in a stare-down for those seats. I perfected the waddle and the look of, "Oh, don't mind me navigating with this wide load." Those seats made the marathon possible—and a precious day with my girl.

But when I got home, I went to my room and cried. It had already changed beyond my control. Would I get through this and ever get back to myself? I sat there a long time trying to sort my bombardment of thoughts.

And just what was "back to myself" anyway? My thoughts were swirling with rapid fire.

Like osmosis that I didn't feel or realize, most times I was wholeheartedly pursuing being a "good mom" but found it was confusing, nebulous, and up to the moment-by-moment definition of others. I held myself to this standard based on observation of what others were doing and saying. No wonder I was lost. No wonder I wasn't sure of my value or how to find meaning every day (more laundry?!? Yippeee! Pick me!). Too conscientious and taking on too much guilt because I wasn't doing it all or because my house was, let's say, in a constant state of "lived in". I mean, I did have so much "free time" on my hands. When I was feeling my worst inadequate self, I would double down: volunteer even more, say yes to whoever needed help, or run this or that event.

During one of these times, our school was having a "travel to different countries" event. Each classroom was a different country. I was asked to make passports to be stamped at each country. Did I just crank out some pocket-sized paper packets? Of course not. I created a passport clone with each country's name, how to say hello, please, and thank you in that language, and added the country flag; and geographical location. It was tons of work, over the top, and I still wonder if they were just trashed moments after the event ended. Crazy. All in. And in deep. Looking for approval in all the wrong places. What's that definition of insanity? Why was I so stuck on this thinking?

Anyway, for round three of the back-to-school days, with my younger son, I showed up even rounder, once again ready for the whole dude experience, quick and to the point. But the real goal with all of them was the bonding of the day, especially over food. He was going into the second grade, and I talked with him about goals, ideas, and what he wanted. I touched on what a new baby would be like and ever so gently danced around the question of whether he would like more info or discussion about how babies are made. (Nope, got it.) "I just want to be sure you don't have any misinformation or confusion, should, say, your friends have maybe offered you definitions for things". (Nope, I'm good.) Check, please.

We carried on with the day, the tasks at hand. He later said, "We can go home when you need to, Mom." Maybe he was clued in to my frequent stops, deep breaths, and using the cart as a walker. It did bum me out that I was not my totally normal, energetic self and, yet again, my child had noticed.

It still felt good to have the one-on-one with each of them. As best I could, I made sure the day was about them and where they were at, addressing any questions, concerns or misinformation and just giving them an idea of what was coming up. Based on the thoughtless comments from other moms, I had no idea what the kids of these moms might be saying to my kids at school. For each of their ages at the time, they seemed to be in good shape to welcome the new baby. I was really trying to join them. I may have forgotten to mention how poopy stuff gets, and how I can be an unrecognizable swamp monster when I go without sleep for too long. Oops.

Back to School

The first day of school arrived and we were all set. We got to the school for all the "first day" pictures with friends, with each other, and solo. It's always such an exciting time. The kids were excited, seeing friends again, buzzing about what teacher they had. In the meantime, I had been lulled into complacency over the summer after not having to see folks at school on a regular basis. So, I completely forgot to gear up for the unsolicited drive-by comments. Maybe at that point I was too tired and slow moving to care.

As I stood there with the parental paparazzi getting my own photos of my superstars, a comment was launched my way: "Oh, wow, you sure are big! You must be due any minute. I forgot about your 'oops' baby! When is the big, tee hee, day?" I turned and said, "Right now. My water just broke on your kid's brand new backpack. Oops." Sorry, just kidding. Fantasy response.

As I turned to say how nice it was of her to notice, and let her know where I was registered for baby gifts, I saw an oasis in the form of my friend walking up with her dog. I smiled and nodded at the woman who'd just called me a house, then I turned to wave to my friend and headed over with gratitude for the reprieve.

Just as I reached my friend, her dog started going after another dog who was also sending off its kids to school. My friend was literally dragged across the wood chips in a quest for a fight. She looked like a professional water skier but wasn't really enjoying the drag. Somehow, I quickly jumped and straddled the dog leash, stopping the dog in its laser focused desire for a rumble. I stepped on the leash to keep him at my side. I may have muttered, "Down, bitch!" My friend hilariously said, "So, the pregnant chick is the only one to come to my aid and corral Cujo?" It was nice to know I could move quickly when I had to. Nice to know in that moment I could trust my instincts, but it was crazy to me how the whole thing really did leave me completely spent.

The next day, we saw a new sign at school that read, "No dogs inside the fence on school grounds". We looked at each other and wondered aloud as to why.

Around mid-September, my friends were joking about maybe doing some jumping jacks or other natural remedies to have the bun be done in the oven, especially since the school cut-off date to start kindergarten (in five years) would be September 16th. In a few years she could start school after having just turned five in time for the deadline rather than waiting for another whole year.

It was triggering me for sure: she could start school in five years, then I could dream about some goals or my personal growth again. But, five long years. And that's IF she were born about three weeks early. Seriously, why even think that way? It comes down to what's best for her. And why did I have to think I couldn't DO anything "serious" or what I was interested in when I would have a newborn, toddler, or preschooler? Why were my paradigm and thinking so stuck? Looking back, why did I define my role as a mom as doing only the things that advanced my kids' lives and assumed there wasn't room for serious consideration for my goals and life direction? Where did these beliefs come from? Underneath it all, why did it seem "not okay" to want what I wanted?

Maybe it was the mistakes I had made while taking care of everything for my family that explained why I already expected to be so overwhelmed. Why I felt so confused, in denial, and discouraged at starting all over. I did too much. I was under the influence of needing to have it perfect. I thought I could head problems off at the pass if I controlled issues from the start. Now add the physical requirements of babies, the lack of sleep (again, my kryptonite), and the worries about handling the whole load. I actually expected myself to not miss a beat with the other kids, because that's what would be expected of me as well. I began to realize, as I journeyed through my brain, that it would HAVE to look different. Maybe, just maybe, some of the ridiculous perfectionism, which wasn't good anyway, would have to go. But I had to recognize and see something before I could address it, deal with it, and decide what I would rather have it look like. I needed to figure out how to manage much better than I had ever before. And I felt lost not knowing how to get there.

Pregnancy brain was in full swing, and hormones were clearly ramping up for the big event. Even so, I used my final weeks before the baby came to map out a six-month, one-year, and five-year vision and goals plan. I researched what it would take, what was realistic, and how to make it happen. Not. I wish.

Instead, I did the tangential nesting type of behavior and set out on a project to create a family history wall with framed pictures: grandparents' and great-grandparents' wedding pictures, family pictures, and our current family picture, plus a couple of nice wooden plaques with sayings on them to complement the look. Big stuff. It took serious effort to keep this new collage of frames aligned, making the pictures straight on the wall. As I finished this project, I looked outside in my yard and wondered if I should just quickly re-landscape everything too.

A Baby Shower, for What? Oh, a Baby

With my mental dismissal of my circumstances came a certain atypical, for me, lack of readiness. With my previous babies, the literal little yellow ducks were all in a row. The bassinet bedding was washed and ready, the crib, prepped. Babies need clothes and binkies and a million diapers. Burp cloths, wash cloths, little baby tubs to clean their little baby stuff. The right gentle baby body washes. Car seats, swings, boppy, playpen, carrying slings, and the list goes on and on.

Pretty much the same list of things that I had outright given away to other expecting moms. My turn was done, and it was a lot of good baby stuff, so... NEXT! I even gave away my breast pump. I certainly never dreamed I would need that incredible contraption again, the one that never failed to bring me to full moo-cow status with desperate dependency. It was my best friend when relief was needed. The breast pump offered me a cross between feeling "freaked out and this seems all wrong" to "if you touch my breast pump I will deliver painful steel-toed kicks to your essential body regions." Unbelievably, I would need one once again.

The kindness of women to the rescue. My friends, fellow soccer moms, and merciful onlookers may have noticed my lack of being in touch with readiness. They would say out loud to each other right in front of me, "She does realize this baby will eventually come, right? Lynn, dear, do you have supplies for the baby?" What baby? I just ate a lot last weekend, and those extra nachos just kicked me in the spleen. They decided a baby shower would do the trick. At least give this little sweetie some clothes and diapers. They also hoped it would give me a kick to be ready for my bonus baby, because ready or not, she was coming.

To this day, I can't thank that group of ladies enough. Sweet friends came to celebrate and offer support. The kind words, the generous gifts, and the sisterhood (that I had been missing) meant and still means the world to me. It reminded me of our common experience, to be able to laugh about some of their awkward stories and hear the crazy comments almost everyone there had heard during their pregnancies, including the incredible intrusiveness of having our bellies caressed by others without permission. And how funny it is to hear men talking about cervical dilation and effacement like it was the latest news.

One woman made a "diaper cake", where she rolled up individual diapers to make layers of the cake, then topped it with cute little washcloths. It was so creative (this was before they were available in the stores), I didn't even want to dismantle it when the time came to use those diapers. I also received so many helpful items that I was truly in need of, not to mention a surprising amount of baby blankets. Even at the time, I thought that someday I would have them all sewn together to make an eclectic "quilt of kindness". I would tell my daughter how important it is to support each other, recognize where someone may be at, and see how you can help, whether that's just by offering a kind word or throwing an awesome baby shower. Or just holding the space for someone.

Funny thing. The same woman was there who'd previously commented about the "sucker" having a baby. We laughed about it then and still do now. And, just maybe, I thought, could I lighten up a bit? Let go of the assaultive comments that piled up, stop taking note, and just release them. Neuter them. Like we tried to do to my husband. But that didn't work entirely either, now did it?

So, their evil plot worked wonders. I brought the loot—the kind and generous gifts—home and slowly went through each. It finally occurred to me I should start setting up for this little girl to enter the world. I was over the moon to meet her and be with her, and love her. I just couldn't shake my thoughts—as it turns out, my illusions—about my mom role. Why did this new child have to equal "stuckness" in my mind? What was I going to do about these illusions, self-imposed restrictions, and implications about advanced maternal age? I was trying to muster up the energy and "right" attitude, but I felt like I was still coming up short for my family, this baby, and myself.

Now What?

One day, about five weeks before D-Day (due date), I woke up with a slight headache. It can be typical in pregnancy to have stuff going on during any given day. This headache, though, started getting much worse. Seriously worse. I had never had a real migraine before and now certainly know to never use the word lightly. I seriously wanted to remove my head. The slightest light was agonizing. My husband was working from home, and I zombie-walked into his office. He quickly got off the phone and asked if I was okay. I said I didn't think so, and… he insisted we go to my doctor. We jumped in the car, and he called on the way to let them know we needed to be seen. We went to see the first wonderful doctor I went to for the sinus infection diagnosis and the reality check on the EPT double blue line. We pulled into a parking space just in time for me to start vomiting. This was not pretty.

I don't even remember everything that happened in the doctor's office or how many tally marks I needed to add to the advanced maternal age comment count. I remember it getting dark and someone requesting me to lie on my side for a shot in the rear. No, not at the back of the office. Bend over and crack a smile. Somehow, I got home and woke up hours later. Apparently, I stopped vomiting at some point. Was this pregnancy-related or some other nightmare? They said I might experience more of these likely pregnancy-related episodes. That's not gonna help: Add migraines to the list of things to fear happening that I can't handle? The kids had also been a bit freaked out, wondering where I was and why I wasn't at the helm. Is she okay? Does this have to do with the baby? What's this all about? Where's dinner?

In the days after this event, I just marched on, that's what moms do. The kids were settling into the start of school, and I was diligently doing the first-of-the-school-year paperwork. You know, the seventeen hours per kid, inputting emergency contact info, the "get to know you" form for the teachers, how much you will pledge to PTA, what areas you commit to volunteer to and when, and permission slips, signing that you agreed to the rules of the school, the school district, and any new, unforeseen rule they may need to make, like if Terminators come from the future. I put my feet up all the while, so I had that going for me. The baby was having a field day in the playground of my organs. It was getting harder to breathe, find a comfortable position, and locate my remaining positivity. Honestly, everything seemed at a low point: my spirits, all my fears (including now of migraines), my mind-set, the baby's head.

The Official Plan

I had my regularly scheduled prenatal checkup, and things were "moving along nicely". The baby's head was down, and all was in alignment. The head being down thing is kind of funny to think about. I mean, there is a lot of pressure down below, and the pregnant woman is aware of it at all times. Yet, it's socially unacceptable to just slip your hand down there and hold things up. I basically had an agreement with my husband and friends that if I stood up and they saw a head, they had to tell me. Don't let me walk around all day not noticing. Like when someone has a piece of string on their butt. Or spinach in their teeth. Because if it were just up to me, with that amount of ongoing downward pressure, I would always guess the head was showing when I stood up. That constant ongoing pressure on my groinage made me categorically certain the birthing process had started without me. Feeling a little less than muscularly solid on the south end from three previous, large, blessed events led me to the conviction that my baby's head was showing. Makes perfect sense.

At the checkup it was finalized: we scheduled the cesarean section for Monday, October 8, 2007. Arrive at 7 a.m. Right. This was really happening, with or without me. It was three-and-a-half short weeks away, and I had better get used to the idea. No turning back. Suck it up, Buttercup.

The Big Day

The Friday before the planned C-section, I was feeling especially breathless. I thought Monday couldn't come soon enough even though I was still in a total panic. By mid-morning Friday, I realized labor had started. There was no denying it, even though my denial was still messing with me. I got stuck in my head and had this huge tennis match: Is this labor? No, it's not. But it could be. But it would be more obvious. But you don't want to get too far down the road if it is—that could mean a lifelong bag... Had I immediately listened more to my heart and intuition and just "momma knowing", there was no question.

She did not stick to the plan. Obviously, from conception on. Recognizing full-fledged labor had jump-started, and once I accepted it, I headed downstairs to let my husband know, Houston, we have a problem. In good old-fashioned *Dick Van Dyke Show*—style, he freaked. Not really that bad, it was just very heightened with all that was at stake. We quickly called the doctor, and they said, "Hold, please." Sure, I'll just cross my legs. After a short hold they urged us to get to the hospital, safely, ASAP. Oooooh, there was something in my chart that indicated urgency. They also said my doctor was in the mountains, and they were trying to contact him to get to the hospital. I'm guessing he must have made notes for them to take extra measures to get him there.

This wasn't expected at all until Monday. He knew the history, circumstances, details, urgency, and everything. I was counting on it going well because he was up to speed on it all. The thought of trying to translate to someone else and have them manage the C-section with more attention to detail rather than default to routine had me panicked. *Okay*, I told myself, *just breathe… breathe… breathe.*

The kids at school! We had no plan in place for this day, Friday, only one for Monday! Operation Call the Village. That was our affectionate name for our friend group of five families because it was clear to us all that it really does take a village with all this kid stuff. Anyway, I started calling friends from the car. First one, no answer—left a heavy breathing message. Second call, no answer, same breathless message. Third, no answer. Looking at EJ, I was like, the kids get out in three hours, but you can't leave me! He said, "No problem, we will get this figured out." We were halfway to the hospital, and my phone rang. It was one of the friends! I tried to talk to her, but I had to keep stopping, like Morse code, between contractions. From her end it must have been pretty funny:

"Hey, the baby is coming! I'm in"—huff, puff… moan… heavy breathing—"labor, apparently. Can you"—huff, puff… moan… silence, breathing—"possibly call the"—huff, puff… moan… breathing—"others to get the" (EJ in the background driving, "Breathe, honey") "kids after school?"

She was on it. I didn't even know who was going where. It was nice to let go and know my children would be very well taken care of. She called the school for us and got a message to each of them that they would be picked up at school by the playground. Thank God I'd filled out the emergency pickup forms for school or I'd have been huffing and puffing with water breaking in the school's front office.

My first-grader and second-grader don't really remember what it was like getting the message that their mom was in the hospital having the baby, but my sixth-grader and his friends remember it vividly. They were at recess, and the teacher came out to tell my son as they were all playing. He later told me they all got so excited and hooted and hollered at the news. They may not have fully understood, but the teacher's enthusiasm and the baby's surprise early arrival got them rallied. They chanted, "Brandon's gonna get a sister, Brandon's gonna get a sister!" How cool was that?

Phew! Now I could focus on the matter at hand. The key was not getting too far along in labor so I could still have a C-section and save my urinary functioning. We checked in, and they put me in a wheelchair. After wheeling by everything so fast that it was a blur, EJ drove me up to the designated area. He smiled sweetly, assuring me all would be okay and that I had this. But I could tell he was nervous too and feeling this intense sense of urgency.

We got into the room, and he started going through the details, all the paperwork, yada, yada, yada, with the staff. A nurse took me to "prep". She helped me into the gown and onto a table. She then said she had to shave the hoo-ha and started very quickly, sloppily, and painfully trying to shave me with a lame little single-blade disposable razor.

I'm like, hold the phone. So, like:

1. This is a C-section, they will cut me higher up so shaving isn't necessary.

2. The thought of the grow-back on that *and* recovering from stitches sounded miserable.

3. Could she be more of a spaz? I understood the sense of urgency, but did I also need to experience her cheese-grater-like attempts at this process?

I put the kibosh on the effort and suggested she consider applying to a landscaping company as a weed-whacker. She did not find that humorous.

She came back in and said she got an "okay" for me not to be shaved (whose body is this anyway?), and to stay on the bed I was on to be wheeled into the delivery room/OR right then. We got in there and the anesthesiologist launched into his bit on what drugs were being used and what would happen. I would not be feeling anything from the neck down. Oh, wow, I fought the panic.

My fears of being incapacitated were kicking in big time, but I decided it would be great to be able to use a toilet for the rest of my life. My whole body was shaking but I focused on pushing those fears aside. To add some additional spice, I was informed that my wrists would be tied down with my arms out to the sides, like on a cross, so to speak. Pregnancy is a sacrifice of the body for sure, but not at that level, if you know what I mean. I was already feeling like I could relate to Mother Mary with the whole immaculate conception part of the story as well. A little more panic showed up, ok, A LOT. EJ was right there at my side, knowing my fears (being paralyzed and alone) and telling me he would never leave for even a second. How blessed am I to have wordless understanding, complete trust and faith, and his ability to talk to me in that moment? "That's right," I said, "WE can do this". But in all candor, I was still silently wondering if I could secretly keep the arm ties a bit loosened, just in case I needed to go all Houdini on that.

The OB doctor entered the room and introduced herself. They didn't get my regular doctor back from the mountains in time. Next level of fear and terror kicked in. Does she know what she's doing with my case? Does she know this situation, how delicate it is? Did she have a good lunch? Is she in a good mood? When was the last fight with her husband? Any extraordinary stress? Has she done this exact procedure before in medical school, or when was the last emergency-C-section-watch-out-for-intricate-extenuating-circumstances surgery?

I shakily asked if she was completely familiar with the circumstances, and the urethra sling complications, and maybe how nervous I was, and is it too late for me to opt out? Maybe give birth another day?

She was saying some words, I think in English, in response. At that point, I could jack myself up more and hyperventilate or go to a place of surrender. I chose the latter. What choice was there?

I also did confirm with the doctor and team that I was taking matters into my own hands via a tubal ligation. That's the female counterpart to the vasectomy, in case you didn't know. Since they were already going in deep, opening up my guts, they were to absolutely dance around those fallopian tubes and cut anything off at the pass, to once again feel like we were "fixed". I would never again be completely sure or trust that "there is NO way" because, yep, I now know things do grow back. In chicks, too.

Okay, so it was officially go time.

Today was the day. No pause button. The first day of my

life being over. Gone, done, stuck, restricted. No give-backs. But did it have to come with so much attention?

I mean, the massive spotlight was so bright, piercing into my eyes. Center stage. I couldn't really see anything, squinting to comprehend what was going on. Then, another searing wave of pain crashed over me. This will be over soon, right? I can handle it, right? I looked to my left and again saw my husband there, and I was encouraged. As they tied down my arms onto boards, straight out to the sides, I felt the full panic of being constrained. Was this really necessary? I'd done this before, but it was so different this time. I'd never been shackled. Because it was an emergency situation, everyone was laser focused and efficient. No time for questions or distractions from the matter at hand.

When the drugs started flowing and everything was a go, they put up a tent-like thing, blocking my vision from my chest down. The procedure was under way. I was no longer feeling contractions, which was weird but expected. Shortly after, I felt a lot of tugging on my body. It was more like "out of body". After a while, they pulled down the little tent and lifted up my sweet baby girl. In one awestruck glance, the doubt, fear, denial, uncertainty, selfishness, and craze in my brain was replaced with that deep, infallible, unconditional love. A mother's love. The doctor said she looked perfect, healthy and beautiful! I just wanted to have her in my arms. That would have to wait though—I was a little tied up.

As they brought her through her first phases of post-tummy life—the Apgar scores, cleanup, checkup—we switched focus to the next procedure, snipping the fallopians. They started the process, lifting some stuff up, moving the pieces of the puzzle, working around the playground of my guts. There was a big, huge light above the operating table in which I could see the reflection of everything they were doing. Very clearly. They had not replaced the little tent thing after the debut of my baby, so I was watching it all. It was super fascinating to watch a procedure again, but then I realized it was MY guts and looked at EJ in that strange, swirly way. I told him I could see the operation, you know, my guts. You want to watch with me? He told the doctor and nurses I was watching, and they got wide-eyed, jumping up and very quickly putting the tent back up. The whole thing seemed completely surreal to me.

The only thing I remembered next was feeling so very tired. Suddenly, uncontrollably, completely depleted.

Where is She?

I woke up later in a quiet, dark hospital room, alone. I guessed that EJ had just stepped out to get something to eat, so he was not there in the moment. Of course, food, right. I was just coming around, and with a few more minutes, I started to figure out where I was. I dared to reach down to my tummy and only found a deflated mushy bag of skin. Interesting. And then it hit me—I had the baby! I looked for the bassinet in the hospital room and didn't see anything. She wasn't cuddled next to me in the bed. So, where was she?

Probably with EJ. Yep, not a food run, he was walking around with her. Wait, that didn't quite make sense either. Just then a nurse quietly peeked in and saw me awake.

"Great!" she said. "Time to get some vitals and check your temp and your wound dressing".

"So, where is she?" I asked shakily.

"Who?" she asked.

Hello… "My baby. Where is she?"

The nurse said, "Oh, no one has talked to you yet?"

Complete drop to a state of pure panic. You know your stomach on those mega-drop roller coaster rides? Exactly that, into a pit of immediate fear. "NO!" I said, just barely maintaining control of my voice.

"Well," said the nurse, "she is in the NICU." (That means alive.) "A doctor will come in and talk to you shortly." (That means in a year.)

"Is she okay?"

The nurse said, "Yes, she is being observed, for some complications." (That means you can't say what, so it could be bad or good. Get someone who can say, before I lose it!)

She said she would like to finish getting my vitals and discuss with me how it would be important to start trying to walk again within a few hours, starting with just a few steps. The sooner I was walking, the quicker I would heal, which would help me get on my way. I'd be walking straight to the NICU in a few minutes, just wait. Of course, not really, but I just needed info, stat!!!

At that moment, the door opened and in came EJ. Thank goodness. What was the deal? He knew how to have some bedside manner (isn't that how we got into this?). Anyway, he immediately told me, she was fine. Nothing was seriously wrong that they could tell. She appeared to have been born with a heart murmur, and they were observing her and getting clarity on what was specifically going on.

"Okay, are you worried?" I asked.

"No," he said, "but it seems serious enough to keep her in the NICU and make sure it's not dangerous."

I guess I could live with that.

My mom-mode muscle-memory was activated and completely reengaged with the next question: "Have they fed her?" Of course, it was too soon to feed her myself, and I was already thinking about the feeding + pooping + frequency = thriving equation that new moms are taught to live by. He assumed they had but didn't know details.

Day turned into night and as the evening carried on, I was in and out of sleep. The pain was starting to ramp up from the cut in the gut, but I wouldn't know the half of that until later. The next morning our pediatrician came in— a familiar face who knew us well. Don't get me wrong, the nurses were absolutely wonderful— kind, caring, patient, and oh so helpful (like getting me to the loo) —but I had known Dr. Max for many years, and we had already been through a lot together.

I think he enjoyed this bonus baby pregnancy quite a lot as well. He said crazy sweet things, like, "You are the best parents to be having more kids!" (Maybe he said that to all the impossibly-pregnant-due-to-vasectomy-grow-back moms). He sat with me and immediately said how sorry he was that she had not been with me for her first night. He was hoping it had worked out differently and felt so bad she was not with me. I felt weirdly logical and matter of fact that it was okay and she was in the best place. Perhaps I feared not knowing if something were to go wrong with her heart. Would I recognize it? Would I know what to do? What if I slept through something happening?

He took plenty of time and carefully explained the details of what was going on, that she had a heart murmur, the specialists were monitoring her, and they would have a clear report shortly. Sometimes they had to repair the heart right away; sometimes it was merely something to monitor. He, with all his years of experience, said he felt this was something that commonly happened. His guess was that she wouldn't have to have surgery. Yikes. Surgery on that little bundle with an even littler heart. With everything she had already overcome to make it here, my money would be on her.

We chatted some more, and he made me feel really good about her birth stats, Apgar scores, and so forth. When he started to leave, I felt a sudden wave of desperation, fear of this potential heart surgery surfacing, and somewhat crazily yelled out, "Will she be okay?" No one would really know, of course, and they would be very cautious talking about it. My outburst was followed by a wave of massive weariness and overwhelm. My body had been through a lot in the last twelve hours. I was trying to wrap my head around what would happen if they came in and said she would need heart surgery. The thought of her having a heart surgery just went to a deep, bone-level worry. This was early on, and I wasn't getting out of bed yet without a lot of assistance. I couldn't do anything, make anything happen, or create a solution, like I was used to doing. I was feeling an unfamiliar helplessness.

The next afternoon another nurse encouraged me again to try to walk as much as possible. The more I could walk, the quicker I would heal, and the faster I would be at home. (Would being at home come with the room service I was enjoying?) I took that as a challenge and started my laps around the floor. At first, from my room to the nurses' station and back, was a crowd-cheering accomplishment. I made three laps the first day. By the next morning I stretched it to the rest of the hallway. I had to stop once or twice in the lap, but by that afternoon I was ready for the hospital hallway walking Olympics. Of course, going for the gold and seeing her from afar in the NICU was incentive enough.

This C-section thing was a new ballgame for me, but I was determined to get back on track, one step at a time.

A bit later, the nurse peeked in saying someone was anxious to see me. I was like, oh boy, who?? (I looked like a train wreck, but I'd just, like, had a baby so it was cool. Why did I even think about that?) Around the corner came the nurse with my newborn, sweet delicious baby girl! I started crying. A deep and visceral, enchanted and enamored, complete love overtook me. It was just like with my first three children, and it's very hard to describe—like saying the biggest and best-est love times a gazillion. It is a deep knowing and bonding and clarity that you will protect, provide for, and love this being forever. And with every ounce of mama bear sauce too.

My denial was finally obliterated, my fears confined. My hope renewed. My gratitude expanded. It meant she was okay enough to travel down the hall. I could hold her up close and no longer have to stare through the window at her twenty feet away in a little cart for a bed.

Since this was the first time I was able to hold her I just sat there and stared. I looked at every tiny thing about her: that sweet little baby nose, her tiny face, the cute hat they put on her to keep her warm. I touched each of her fingers and enjoyed her itsy-bitsy hands. Her diminutive ears were the cutest. Those delicious cheeks! She smelled of innocence. I literally looked at every pore on her face. I held her body close, still reconciling that less than twenty-four hours before she had been inside of me, sharing the same blood system and playing sternum soccer. And then it happened...

She opened her eyes. She checked me out. Although her full vision would be coming around fully in the next few days, I held her close up and kept staring at her. And she just stared back at me. Wouldn't it have been cool to understand her thoughts in that exact moment? Were they similar to those in the book, *Are You My Mother*? Or maybe, the slightly more painful version in my case, *Are You My Grandmother*? However, surely, she was like, "Yep, things grow back, and here I am." Perhaps with some "get over it"? I was finally SO completely grateful. I just wanted to take care of her no matter what. Sleeplessness? Still not my favorite, but I'm in. Breastfeeding with my forty-three-year-old boobs 'till they are at waist level? You bet. Teaching her life? I can't wait. Reading to her the books I now know by heart? Bring it! Worrying about her when she is sick and when friends are rough? Trying to get it right for her best life? Yes. All of it.

I beat myself up for a while over why I couldn't just remember this magical moment of bonding and the joy of it to get me through my doubt during the pregnancy. To get me past myself. To stop worrying about the physical fears. The nagging questions like, how am I going to possibly manage all this?

But I also didn't realize the illusions I was living under. I didn't know what I didn't know, like how I narrowly defined my role as mother and stay-at-home mom in a way that limited me. How did I ever arrive at my thinking of having to do it all and make it perfect? Why did I think I couldn't pursue my dreams (or have any for that matter) because I was so tied down? What gave me an all or nothing attitude?

As I was lost in thought, my other kids and husband came in the room. It was so cute to see two of them in soccer uniforms. How could I have forgotten they had games that morning? I had to laugh out loud as my "on top of everything" self met with the "letting it all go" self, and I wondered how they would be getting along in the months to come.

I handed the baby to EJ for the first time. Just seeing

his large, caring, loving self, holding that precious bundle made me, well... you guessed it... cry. Tears of joy that would not stop. He was crying too, so I had no choice in the matter. Then our oldest sat on the other bed in the room. My husband ever so sweetly placed her in his nervous sixth-grader arms. He was an instant natural. There was an eye-lock and seeming immediate bond. I have the pictures to prove it. Next, my second son took a crack at holding this wee bundle. He nailed it, too. So precious to see him really grasp that this little creature was hanging out in my belly and to watch him slowly and gently touch her little fingers. Lastly, my (newly minted middle) daughter, six years old at the time, anxiously awaited her turn. She snuggled next to me and took her sister in her arms. Seeing the sisters together, yep, you guessed it, made me cry.

She was really captivated by her new sister, and I believe she felt the same awe; this little human is the one from your belly? The one I felt kick? Dang, she's adorable but still not getting my room. They were beautiful together.

Now, I could declare, once and for all, here we had it: our family unit. Done. Complete. Amazing. Reframed. Vasectomy failure acknowledged—check. Moving forward, relying on the tubal ligation—check. That was the plan. You know about plans though...

It's funny how sometimes you feel like you want the world to come and visit you in the hospital! They must see this angel. Everyone must see this miraculous creation RIGHT NOW! Come ye, see what I have brought forth!! Some wonderful friends did come and visit. Super sweet. And mercifully, they didn't stay long. I really was winded from my training (laps around two nurses' stations now). She was rooming with me at this point and beyond; all feedings were up to me now. So, okay, let the sleeplessness begin. Mush-headedness would be the friend that visited for the foreseeable future. But she was with me now, and I was blissed out. And, blessed—we got the word that heart surgery wouldn't be necessary at this point. Nothing else mattered.

Lactation "Support"

It's really not a complaint—about receiving support and counseling for lactation. Looking at the nurses' and consultants' side of things, they surely have a lot to manage. They probably have a whole variety of "welcomes" from patients/new moms depending on what the mom's state is in the moment. Sometimes, though, it seems like they pop in the room at the craziest times. Such was the case with our lactation consultant. I was pretty out of it. Sweet girl had been up plenty in the night (you know the challenge of just getting back to sleep and you hear; wa… wa… wahhhh… waaaahhhhh!), about every two hours. Plus, I had lingering worries about what to look for if this heart murmur thing were to go south.

As I was feeling a bit like a wrung-out dishrag, the consultant entered the scene, eager to educate me. Address concerns. Outright fondle my udders. I had already started to nurse, and it was going just okay since her first days of feeding in the NICU had been with a bottle. Bottles are just easier, and at all ages we humans opt for the easy route. Now the work was syncing us up, and she was having second thoughts. Thankfully, this was number four on the lactation rounds, and I was not too concerned. We'd get there, but not on anyone else's schedule.

The consultant bounced in with pamphlets and described

the process and what to expect the first few days before my full milk came in—what to look for, how to know the baby is getting what she needs. How to supplement with bottles (interesting). What to look for in my body as my full milk came in—had my own inside joke at the reminders of that painful process that they don't really talk about.

The consultant then informed me she would like to "have a look" and see about getting the baby latched on. I tried to let her know I was good, that I had experience, and since the baby was sleeping, I would cut off her arm if she woke her. Somehow that didn't come across, and she was hanging out with my "girls" before I knew it. "They look great," she said. My husband was in the room then, and we looked at each other, trying not to laugh hysterically like fourth-graders. I would not have been able to stop. She actually evaluated my nipples (remember back when you were warned about the TMI?). "Oh—very good!" she exclaimed. I was like, damn right. My over-tired self thought (and wanted to blurt out), "How are yours, miss cold-handed intrusive-pants?"

Then she started going into more detail, and I just outright asked if there was a hotline for questions if I ran into problems. This was my fourth child, after all, and my experience should carry me through. She then said, number four? Yep, things do grow back. Oh, no, not that whole explanation. She said, "Wow, great. Now I just need to see the baby latch on successfully for my paperwork."

Oh, why didn't you say so—whatever you need. Seriously!? I have a statement for your paperwork. And perhaps a gesture. But apparently, she was part of the reporting necessary for our release from the hospital, so I danced: Awaken baby. Intro breast. Have strange lady grab breast. Heave-ho into baby's mouth at perfect point of her crying (like when you are timing to jump into a jump rope). Baby handled the shock and decided she liked food. Way to go, sweetie. Done. Write it up.

Now, I have tremendous gratitude for the process being a relatively easy one for me. I know it's not always a given. Even if you manage the Herculean effort of syncing mom and baby, there does have to be enough milk, which is a guess. You can see the contents of a bottle. You can't see how many ounces are in a boob. I realized when I had my second son in Germany that I was blessed in this area. While he was under observation, I had to pump the milk and they would bring it to him. This included, the middle of the night and at all times of the day, meeting up with all the other women in the pump room. We all spoke different languages and were too focused to chat it up anyway. I would get there, attach the electric milker, start mooing, and let it rip. A few minutes later I would have four to five ounces—plenty. I would follow the cleanup and labeling instructions and head out. Not sure how to say "damn showoff" in Arabic or German, but I may have heard something of the sort after a pumping session.

Bottom line, I could trust myself, my knowing and my experience on this.

Time to Go Home

We were released from the hospital five days after arriving in such a rush. I packed our few things from the room, and my two-wheeled chariot arrived for the evacuation. As I reflected, those last days or last weeks of pregnancy would have been a great time for a wheelchair. I made a mental reminder to offer pregnant ladies a seat whenever I could. How nice it was to be rolled along, holding my sweet girl with her designated pink hat.

The awesome older volunteer ladies stopped us along the way and just crooned over her. That was so cool. I looked at them and thought, they did it. They probably raised kids and lived to tell. They probably have amazing stories, too. Man, would I love to hear them. And they may or may not have done it like I have so far. They had different challenges and surely stories of triumph as well. I felt a change bubbling. Or a desperate need to change how I went about this thing. This raising of kids, this "growing up" a family. I needed it to include a growing up of me also. As I ruminated on these thoughts, I felt excited, somewhat weary and blissed out. EJ was taking care of the discharge papers, the bill, and proof that we had a car seat (and were not morons), and handling all the checking-out issues—thank goodness. I sent a quiet prayer up for single moms.

Delivering a New Me

How was this going to work now? Get focused and mother on? Of course. But… nothing was the same.

When the dust settled, there was an inertia to numbly go back to the sameness of everyday life—momming just like before and figuring out the new normal now with four children: the routines, the same ol' ways of doing things. Wondering if I was doing it right and being judged either way. There was a dullness and ache. Been there, done that. I could do plenty of it in my sleep—and kind of had been for years.

I could've carried on, working hard to meet artificial demands, focusing on the job at hand each day, and reconciling the idea of never quite measuring up; shamed by the "shoulds." I could've kept trying to convince, prove, argue, and get agreement on how I worked hard too and that my job mattered, all the while feeling shamed by my secret feelings and fears that maybe it didn't really matter at all. Maybe I'd just settled.

Things just couldn't stay the same. There was a new, tingling, tiny internal voice that could not be put in a time-out. It started slow and meek, but it grew. I tried to sleep it off, but it stuck around. I wasn't sure what it was trying to say, what it was trying to tell me. I wasn't used to listening.

One day a few months postpartum, I was driving home after a PTA meeting. The baby was in the back, nodding off in her car seat. For the fifth day in a row, I was noticing so many stuck tumbleweeds—wedged in fences and ditches, under some cars, they were everywhere. They must have been tumbling along their path, blown around by the wind, and just got hung up. Hmmm. Weird. They really were everywhere. I mean, it was normal for Colorado to have tumbleweeds, but this seemed unusually infested.

When I got home and stepped out of my car, I had that sticky feeling of my shoe being suctioned to the garage floor. Yep, a big-ass wad of gum stuck to the bottom of my shoe. That's gonna be a bear to rip off, I thought. So, I headed into the house, mucked-up shoe in hand, my sleeping baby in her car seat cradled in my left arm, purse and notebook and travel tea mug in my right—the proverbial picture of a mom needing one or two more arms. I shuffled in and did the little foot push on the door to close it.

Next thing I knew, I couldn't move. I was trapped. It seemed my purse strap was hooked on the outside door-knob. I was pinned, and my left shoulder, fully supporting the weight of the baby and car seat, was already thanking me in its special way with shooting pain. Shimmying to set everything down, I maneuvered out. I then gingerly carried the baby to her crib silently begging she would somehow transfer and stay asleep for just a little while… *Pleeeease?!*

As I came back to start the gum-removal process, I passed by my collage of family pictures (from my nesting efforts months ago) and noticed, yet again, that one frame that always needed adjusting. I realigned it with a couple of fingers, laughing to myself, knowing I would walk by it again and it would again need to be straightened out.

Right between the eyes, it hit me, an overwhelming epiphany—and hilarity—overcame me. Stuck tumbleweeds, the gum wad, being trapped by my own doorknob, and going by the same set of pictures that always needed adjusting? What the heck? Could there be a message here? Was someone trying to tell me something or show me something such as maybe, just spit-balling here, my mindset being stuck? Could it be?

The blaring alarm clock of my life was ringing, and there was no snooze button. No rolling over and saying, "Five more minutes." It was time to own myself, to take a hard look at my choices and thought patterns, to examine the good and the bad. It was time to ditch the sad and often pathetic victim thinking, and instead, acknowledge the wisdom and pure awesomeness of what I had learned, experienced, navigated and built as a mom. It was time to give myself credit for what I had already created and look forward to all the new possibilities. It was time to realize that personal growth wasn't just for corporate executives, entrepreneurs, and college students. It hit me that it was absolutely for us all, and certainly for those of us growing others who would be fully unleashed on society someday. It was for moms and dads, the ones who were very much at the heart of the matter of that child-raising gig. It was time to wake up.

As my mindset shifted, I could see that a bonus baby at forty-three years of age, was a great gift—the opportunity to rewatch the same movie over again, to catch so much more, and to appreciate the advantages of my experience. To be far more present in the moment, becoming the intentional creator of my life, not just its servant. My fourth child's arrival six years after my youngest and twelve years after my oldest gifted me the chance to step back and observe. So what if I was a little bit older? Maybe it was time to reframe the negative "advanced maternal age" and realize it was really *advanced maternal wisdom*? I began to give myself the space to pay attention to "nudges" (like tumbleweeds) and to see things through a different lens, things I hadn't seen before. I was catching different nuances, questioning the heck out of stuff, and looking at the picture of my life with a whole new awareness, especially my role and the expectations of "Mom". I was releasing the idea and implied expectations that I had to always show up with "the perfect cupcake", or else.

Instead of staying asleep and accepting "that's the way it is, that's how things are done", I was awakening to ask a slew of new questions, like:

Who am I becoming?
What (the heck) am I doing? Why?
What is required of me compared to what I require
of myself?

When did I decide to be such a victim weenie? I mean, geez, I got to stay home and raise my children, for goodness sake. Lack gratitude much? But why? Why so unvalidated? Why did I even look to others for that? Why question my worth and contribution to society? Why did the definition of that have to come from someone else? What does faith mean in all this, and what did I believe? Why did I allow misaligned and often ignorant comments into my thinking at all? After all, they weren't mine to own. I began to really relate to a three-year-old's way of walking through the world, "why, why, why"?

My sister-in-law would often come to mind. She was gone; her life here was done so suddenly, it was so brief, relatively speaking. Would she have done anything differently if she'd known how young she would pass on? What if the same went for me?

Why was I not pursuing awesomeness and fulfillment every day for my family AND myself? Why was I living according to expectations and zombie-ing through each day? What if my life was suddenly cut short like hers? What would I do differently?

The biggie—how had I "lost myself" when I once believed that would never happen?

So many questions, so little time. It was time to rethink everything, and it was not only okay to do that but also an imperative. In hindsight (I always look forward to hindsight), I believe there was a reason my bonus baby was sent to me at that beautiful age and stage of my life. It launched me into seeking out different ways of thinking, searching for new experiences, and creating new paths to a new me. My newly formed habit of questioning became an internal self-check. I questioned how I did things, with a greater awareness of my thoughts and beliefs, giving clarity to the motives behind my actions. Is this true to me? Is this aligned with who I am, what I want? "This is how it's always been done" met with "Who says?"

I unearthed the illusions I'd been living. I don't know if I ever would have questioned my auto-piloted life without the miraculous arrival of my unexpected bundle. Catching and understanding more of the scenes in this movie of life,

I allowed myself to stop, get centered, be open and willing to think. To catch the negative thought pattern cycles and choose new ones. I was amazed at what I discovered when I pulled my head out of the sand and looked around. Slowly but surely, I started to learn, see, and grow anew.

I decided— 'cause, like, it's actually my decision— to get intentional about who I was becoming and to be clear on who I was already. I started on a journey of illusion-shifting, reframing, challenging my beliefs, thoughts, routines, and expectations of myself. I love how Brené Brown calls her personal adventure her "~~breakdown~~ spiritual awakening" because I feel it frames it up so perfectly for me as well, even though we had different ways of getting there. Mine included the surprising arrival of a new human, and Brené's was a massive, life-changing reevaluation via her cutting-edge research.

My path back to myself and to mom-wholeheartedness, was a full-out exploration of past, present, and "what now". I was asking so many new questions and processing life with a new trust and belief in myself, instead of seeing what everyone else was doing or worry about what others would think. I didn't know exactly where I was headed, but I knew I was on a new path to figure it out for me and to reconcile this role of "Mom", all while smashing some old notions along the way.

I happily embarked upon this journey (although not always so easy to take an honest look at yourself and commit to change), and to this day I choose to create the life I desire, even with the unknown, unexpected and sometimes big curveballs life has to offer. I face challenges differently and I'm more aligned with myself. This art of momliness is of my own creation, evolving from my daily choices. I am grateful for my deep and transformative breakthroughs, the true and lasting lightbulb moments along the way. With awareness, soul-searching, self-reflection and learning new practices, it all delivered the new me.

MY KEY AHA'S TO AWAKENING:

Exploring and accepting self-worth

Growing through the art of self-reflection

The power of thoughtful rituals

A deep dive into evaluating my beliefs, literally taking inventory and cleaning house

The synergistic effect of having a village

Soul level self-trust

The eye-opening process of unlearning

What gratitude really is and how I infuse it in everything

The journey to the other side of judgment, via vulnerability

The joy-inducing quest of "lightening up" and humor procurement

Core level well-being

EXPLORING AND ACCEPTING SELF-WORTH

Ah, worthiness. I wondered what that was all about and why is it so hard for most of us to grasp, accept, have and sustain. Why is questioning our self worth ingrained in us, especially as women, from an early age? The acceptance of our worthiness is vital because it is the mother of confidence, authentic relationships, self-trust, fulfillment, life's path and purpose, and so much more. As I went through my awakening I found a "you should feel worthy cause you are" mantra, seemingly everywhere. This wasn't a negative "should-ing" to simply try to *feel* worthy, it was more the nudge of encouragement to embrace, no, make it part of the definition of who I am. An understanding that worthiness is intrinsic to the soul.

I experienced and pursued numerous activities and discussions on self-worth. Listened to Ted Talks, read books, went to see speakers and looked for it in personal development. Through all of this, one of the keys to my transformation was learning to hear my thoughts, my real time self-talk. To personify it separately from me and evaluate whether this talk was true to me? Was it ok to say or think this about myself? If someone was saying this to my best friend, would it be ok? If not, I would stick up for my friend, right? I learned to stick up for myself, I was my own friend. And it felt refreshingly good.

This expansion of my awareness and claiming my own worthiness (and celebrating everyone else's) encouraged my path to renewal. Tending to my mind, body and spirit. Nourishing my world to be able to give not from a barren place of exhaustion and discouragement but from whole-heartedness. Taking my tattered self-image to a place of acceptance of my worth was like the wonder of the changing seasons. Radiating who I am, comfortable in that skin, became my evidence of self-worth and self acceptance. Renewed daily.

"Things in this life can be fairly uncertain, so it's best to become certain about yourself."

— Lynn Bodnar

GROWING THROUGH THE ART
OF SELF REFLECTION

"Ask better questions and you get better answers" says Tony Robbins. As I began to make new choices, and earnestly open to constant questions and checking in with my heart, I began living with a new clarity and fortitude. For the first time, perhaps, I gave focused consideration to the question, Who am I really? Having not allowed myself to stop and think, especially in the present moment, how could I expect to adjust or be aligned? Create happiness? Or to know what resonated with me? Instead of just how I'm supposed to be, like on social media. Keeping the question handy—what do I require of life vs. what life requires of me?

Evaluating without self-condemnation or habitual pessimism (a very important allowance). It occurred to me that I had conformed to how the culture prescribes the role of mom. I realized I had diminished my "mom knowing" and stripped away my trust in my natural intuition that ultimately served me best. Tapping into that heart-centeredness included listening to my intuition, not just brushing it off, validating my mom-radar and going with it, and giving myself permission to be wrong as well (choosing to learn from it).

Just when I thought I was doing pretty well at being aware of my thoughts, reflecting and choosing an intentional, heart-guided life, I was put to the test. And it shook me to my core.

I attended an event called Elevation, put on by Tiffany Peterson. She is amazing, and she brought on several "guest stars" who were beyond the price of admission. One speaker was Chad Hymas. He's a Hall of Fame Speaker and was named one of the 10 most inspirational speakers by the Wall Street Journal (you'll know why if you ever get to see him). He's a quadriplegic, confined to a wheelchair as a result of an accident on his elk ranch.

The way he engaged the crowd was mesmerizing, and I was fully locked in. Considering the notion that I may show up to life more paralyzed than he does was an interesting mind bend, and I could see where it had been true for me. And then it happened... I felt it coming too.

He had two volunteers join him on stage. Their instructions were to each open a bottle of water and take a drink. They both easily and quickly did as they were instructed and set the water bottles back down on the stage. Then he told them to take another sip, but, oh yeah, you can't use your hands or arms at all.

When the volunteers had first arrived on stage, I had already put down my notebook and pen. I can't say how I knew—guess my heart already did. As the two struggled to try to corner their water bottles and somehow navigate the cap, I knew I was supposed to get up and help. Quietly and efficiently, just get up and help them and sit back down. My heart was screaming, "Get your butt up and do it! GO!"

But my head was rationalizing. What if he is making some other point that I ruin? What if I look totally stupid? What if he yells at me and I'm embarrassed in front of 350 people? What if I'm making this about me (look at me helping, aren't I so righteous)?

Out of the corner of my eye I noticed he started to shake his head, and I let it all go, jumped up, and headed toward the person on the left side of the stage. Right then another woman and I almost collided heading up to the stage. As I got close to help the volunteer, Chad boomed, "Stop!" Oh no! My worst fears. I'll pretend I'm someone else if he asks my name. Jennifer Aniston, that's who I am, yeah, that will work. Total resemblance.

He proceeded to point out that after talking about showing up paralyzed in our lives, focusing on ourselves instead of what's right in front of us, and not pursuing life from the heart, only two people in this whole room chose not to let these two volunteers just struggle on alone. My fears subsided for a moment. Phew, I felt awkward but at least I wasn't "wrong" (as judged by… ?).

However, there was a side effect. Reflecting later that night, I outright cried, disappointed in myself that I hadn't jumped up immediately. There was a reason my notebook was already on the floor. My intuitive heart already knew. Here I was thinking that I was all living heart-centered and self-aware, and the plain truth was I was still worried about all those other factors, including prioritizing my own embarrassment over helping someone in need. My head bossed me around with its rationale in the moment, and then I beat myself up for not listening immediately to my heart or intuitive voice.

I've learned to not two-by-four myself so badly for things like that. I honor that I even noticed the scenario and now work on being more present to my heart's nudges. Perfect? Heck, no. Progress? Thankfully. Through self-reflection, honest assessment and honoring myself in the process.

"The closer you come to knowing that you alone create the world of your experience, the more vital it becomes for you to discover just who is doing the creating."

—Eric Micha'el Leventhal

THE POWER OF THOUGHTFUL RITUALS

I had been under the illusion that self-care was selfish or that it would be wrong to ever put myself first, and it was pretty hard-core stuck in my thinking. Make it about me? I'm the mom, I chose this, continue on and don't complain (or express my needs). Identifying my identity crisis, I realized I was pretty far gone down the hole of this way of thinking and didn't do much to regularly take care of myself. More like, grind myself into the ground and with my last breath ask what everyone wanted me to make for dinner. Cue the eye roll.

As times have changed, though, we all have at least heard of self-care to some extent. It's gotten plenty of press (maybe too much, diluting its importance?), but hearing about it is different from knowing why and how to incorporate doing things to take better care of yourself. Just hearing about it also doesn't help you know the power of consistently practicing self-care.

I resonated with having practices and routines that gave me a reminder of who I am and who I was choosing to become. Like how regular mediation provides well being, grounding, clarity and balance. Demonstrating loving care for myself showed me the manifestation of my worthiness. Supportive rituals have given me a better ability to navigate life, with all I can control and all that I cannot. They offer an invitation to creativity. Which brings a serenity as well (and who doesn't feel even 1% calmer in a bath—even if it's

quarantined off with "stay out" police scene yellow tape?).
I began to feel more wholehearted in my purpose and my
role as a mom, by providing myself the space to marinate in
positivity instead of worrying about the next spill to clean
up or the next debate to face, ending in "cause I said so."
That would still be there, but I would show up differently,
"in" myself, intentional, with a certain peace. Bottom line,
thoughtful rituals and practices are the beautiful reminder
that I am to be taken care of too.

Each person is different and can flow with a universe full
of possible ways to create your own resonating rituals. There
are an endless amount of things to do for oneself. I have
rituals for how I start my day and how I end my day. Planning
my sleep is important to me. I have developed my own
forgiveness ritual which is particularly helpful. The practice
of intentionality is an ongoing priority everyday. Joy-listing,
how I play, space to be with others, activities that matter to
me (like reading) and so much more. It's like I discovered a
portal to a new me.

"Taking care of yourself through thoughtful
rituals ratifies your worthiness and expands your
possibilities to thrive."

— Lynn Bodnar

A DEEP DIVE INTO EVALUATING MY BELIEFS, LITERALLY TAKING INVENTORY & CLEANING HOUSE

Beliefs are inward convictions, feelings of certainty about what something means. I would add to this definition, "habitual, default and perhaps unexamined thought processes." I had certainly motored on through life with my unexamined and ingrained beliefs up until the bonus baby curveball. Thankfully, I began to question…

What were my beliefs around the role of mom? Where did they come from? What did I just do without even thinking about, out of default? Why did I accept certain attitudes or activities as like, yep, that's my job, I have to do it or who else would? Why did I buy into other's insecurities and sometimes panic that there is only one right way, don't screw it up? Including if you don't sell your soul (and bank account) to sports, etc, your kid will never be in the club, so to speak.

What other beliefs had I been blindly operating on that needed to be questioned? I began journaling and asking myself so many questions that I created my own inventory to give raw, real, guts-out answers. Not for anyone else to speak into or question; solely for me. Not to gather up my viewpoints for discussion, purely a vehicle for me to return to me. For my own clarity about what I truly believe and why. It's like a door opened and I walked through to see, for one thing, that I was steeped in my stuckness (or the belief that I was stuck). Which attracted more of that negativity, with more evidence of my inadequacies to wallow in. Which in turn brought resistance, oversensitivity, and a subconscious buy-in to things like being tagged as the "just" in just a stay-at-home-mom.

Releasing some beliefs brings you to a new level, a new awareness and a new way of being. My belief "a-ha-ing" caused face scrunching, jaw dropping, and uncontrollable smiling—serious face shifting. I wonder if I looked at all like my son's face the moment he totally busted me putting money under my daughter's pillow and extracting a dead tooth?

See, one night I was up most of the night with the baby. At about 6:30 a.m. I wearily zombied (yeah, that's a verb) down to my bedroom for maybe a 15-minute snooze before having to wake the rest of the kids for school. As I walked by my daughter's bedroom door, I remembered she had lost a tooth the previous day. Crap. Panic. I ran downstairs and anxiously searched for a dollar or something of value. I found a wadded-up dollar in the bottom of the dryer—score! I ever so quietly tiptoed into her room in good Grinch-like fashion. Just as I was stealthily making the exchange of money for dental matter, I heard a slight, "Mom? What? You're the Tooth Fairy?" I whipped around only to see my son taking it all in. Can't lie, I thought. I could tell by his face, he'd seen too much.

Well, this is it, then. I told him to go wait for me downstairs. I finished the deed of deception and tried to think of the best scenario. I asked what he saw. He thoroughly explained. I asked what he thought. He said, "Well, seems like you are the Tooth Fairy. Makes sense. And now I'm guessing you are Santa and the Easter bunny too." The dominos fell quickly. It was fascinating to be able to watch his very thought process and reactions to big changes in his beliefs in the "realness" of the Big 3. He was pretty chill and handled it well. He even had a little head-nodding realization type of chuckle. I reassured him he'd still get all the goods and now he could be a helper and enjoy bringing the fun to his sisters. "Sounds like fun, Mom. I'm in." How cool.

Of note was how he let go of those big beliefs fairly smoothly, fairly quickly. He just seemed to be able to flow with the life-changing acceptance that these guys were not the real deal. That part of his life completely changed as he knew it. He's like that. Maybe he had already been pondering. It was a real contrast to my clinging to outmoded, erroneous, unhappiness-making beliefs about how society frames up the role of mom and the required perfection. And how convinced I was that I didn't measure up.

"I'm forever impressed how much I can
learn from my kids."

—Lynn Bodnar

-ᘒ-

THE SYNERGISTIC EFFECT OF
HAVING A VILLAGE

As Brené Brown says, we are wired for connection and belonging. We are meant to live in a village, to have and give support, to benefit from our human interactions. To learn from each other and not go down this road of life alone. They say people with strong friendships live longer, but more importantly, happier. All the more true for moms with the often times isolating job of caring for children. Plus, like in every job or experience, it's important to have those around you who really understand where you are at — they "get" you. You don't have to explain the agony of sleeplessness or frustration of a circular teenage conversation. Your mom village laughs with you, often times with both of you in tears that flow down your leg.

This became abundantly clear to me with the bonus baby. I had friends who stuck it out with me, I had some who didn't have the patience and I became clear that no one really understood the shoes I was walking in. To hang out with moms in a newborn or breastfeeding group would certainly have been good, but none aligned because I was so much older. The connection just didn't flow, even though I tried. Also trying to keep up with the mom groups of my older kids always felt like I was spinning my wheels, too slow, and often said "go ahead without me." I often felt left out.

It is hard sometimes. You move. Your baby status changes. Your marital status changes. Your career changes.

Your mindset changes. What occurred to me, as I embraced all this change because it wasn't going anywhere, was to stay open. Open and willing to make the effort to try different things, new and diverse experiences. Meeting new people and braving the awkward "ask" to meet sometime for tea. Then being true to myself on what I enjoyed and where I could find that true belonging and support. Where the true me fit in. I could honor my own boundaries in a new way, knowing that if something feels like it wasn't right for me, then it wasn't. Move on. (And KNOW that nothing was wrong with me).

The synergistic effect of having a village comes when you reach out, find your person, persons, groups, village that has the effect of bringing you to your highest self, validates and up levels you. For me, this came about as I chose to join an inner circle group as a quest for personal development. I found the beautiful timing and blessing of a unique and phenomenal group of women, all at their own place, as we came together and grew together. Giving and receiving. Each finding the blessing of belonging.

I was convinced of the importance of having my village and ever open to the ebb and flow of it. From where I'm at, being able to receive, and from where others are at and how I could contribute.

"Friendship is born at that moment when one person says to another: 'What! You too? I thought I was the only one.'"

— C.S. Lewis

SOUL LEVEL SELF-TRUST

I found self-trust was the offspring of the true acceptance of my self worth. The idea of trusting little old me started in my brain through my ongoing questioning, enjoying my answers and then it migrated to my heart. From there I "epiphanied"—don't believe everything you think, but if your heart speaks, definitely listen up. And, always invite your heart to speak. That's when it becomes soul level.

Trusting myself, my judgment, my decisions and the like didn't mean I had to get things right all the time. I released the idea and immense pressure of feeling that I had to be perfect. I could make mistakes. I would make mistakes. It's what I did with those mistakes. It's *how* I failed and where it took me with new intentionality and purpose. Instead of listening to others and living the faults they pointed out, I would choose instead to continue trusting myself even in the face of being wrong. It only meant that I was getting closer to that goal. It also gave me the opportunity to demonstrate to my children how to handle failure and making mistakes, with ownership and grace. With my belief that if I wronged someone, I would sincerely apologize, ask how I could make it right, do that and then I could release it. Even if that person chose not to forgive. That wouldn't be mine to change, that would be up to them to own.

My slow and steady growth of self trust felt great. I still had the trepidatious feelings around failure but now I knew what they were and how to navigate them.

So, a poignant day came to test out some of my new self trust. "I trust myself and believe in what I'm doing" was my mantra. My bonus baby was about three or four years old. That day, she just woke up defiant and pissy. Everything was a struggle. She even argued about going to the bathroom—after holding it all night. Breakfast was a battle; brushing teeth was a fight. Then it came to getting dressed; she simply refused. With her foot firmly planted on the ground, I was like, "Okay, then," and secretly cheered because she would be facing the natural consequences of her peers asking her why she was in PJs. We went to school, late of course, Sleeping Beauty jammies and all.

As we checked in with the teacher, I just casually said to my daughter, "Love you, honey, see you in a bit."

The teacher, dripping with condescension, said, "Why is she in PJs? It's not pajama day, you know."

I responded, "That's what she chose today. Is there a problem? Is she still welcomed?"

"Well… I guess so," she replied, oozing with judgment, and adding, "Oooooh, Lynn. You should really know better by now."

I smiled a couldn't-care-less smile and turned on my heel. Quoting Buzz Lightyear: "Not today, Zurg." I nearly skipped out of the building, pretty proud of myself. Formerly I would have been bumbling an apology, embarrassed and irritated with my daughter. But this day, my inner peace was palpable. I wanted to bottle that and be able to drink it for the times I was less than fortified with this certitude, because those days would still happen. But for this day, I was in the zone, busting the groveling, apology-required illusion.

I became regularly honest with myself, stepping back to ask important questions. What's the situation here? Where does this align with my beliefs? What do I know? What do I or we need? What is the impact?

That day, I shifted the illusion that I reported to the teacher or that I had to impress or please her. I went from my heart, and trusted what I thought was best for us for that day. Right or wrong, it would never really be wrong because I intentionally chose. At a minimum, I would at least learn something, benefit from feedback, fortifying myself in the process. And worst case? Being sent home would be a great lesson for my daughter and perhaps the crab-a-thon teacher to reflect on as well.

I realized that I could indeed trust my choices even though that self- doubt had lingered and had been built into my thinking over time, from what I carried with me, from the parenting environment around me, and from those traps I created all by myself. Committed instead to questioning, opening to possibility and consulting my thoughts and feelings. My heart directed, empowered and welcomed new habit of self-trust.

"The privilege of a lifetime is being who you are."

—Joseph Campbell

THE EYE-OPENING PROCESS
OF UNLEARNING
& ILLUSION SHIFTING

How do you know what you don't know? And when you are presented with new learnings and "a-ha's", are you open to unlearning? Illusion shifting? This is the road I found myself traveling, experiencing the awakening of how my notions of the role of mom had been influenced and determined, with or without me. I started to think about why I thought moms were solely responsible for most things, how they are "supposed" to show up, how the role was talked about, portrayed in most movies and tv and so forth. Like in the movie, *Bad Moms*, when they were taking the afternoon off to go to a movie and one mom feels it necessary to ask, "is this ok? are we allowed to do this?" I noted where my examples came from and my ingrained perceptions, and some went pretty far back.

I could see where I had bought into the idea of perfect parenting, controlling outcomes, and let's be honest, sometimes judging other moms to try to feel better about my own perceived and suppressed inadequacies. I worried about what others thought and what they were doing for their kids that I was missing out on. It began to occur to me that perhaps many moms were wearing masks of expectations. Here we moms were all at the same masquerade party playing a pretend game, pretending not to notice.

I further noticed my misalignment. Clinging to some notion that I needed an outside paid job to be validated. But I didn't decide to find an "appropriate" job, I just worried about it, and then battled with the argument in my head whether I could manage it all and maintain the homefront.

I got to a place where I asked myself, "If I believe X then why do I do Y?"

I decided to remove the habit of looking for approval and validation in all the wrong places. It always started and ended with me. My "in the moment" revelations became quite interesting to me as well. For example, I invited my own personal thought-checker into my brain every day. One day, mid-metamorphosis, I was getting out my flour sifter to make a traditional gingerbread recipe from my great-grand-mother. I pulled out the ragged piece of waxed paper that I would use and replace in the sifter each time. It had to be at least 5 years old—okay, really 10. I stood there for a long time just looking at this overused piece of waxed paper. I wondered, why do I do this? Why do I keep this holed-up waxed paper, sift the dry ingredients on it over and over, and hope it gets into the bowl without too much spilling out of these worn holes and tears? Because that's what my mother did. And her mother as well. So, I did it without question or thought. Until now. Why not use my flexible plastic cutting board without a single hole that I can wash each time? Huh. How about that—innovation with contemplation.

Jarred back to the present, I heard, "Mom, you actually gonna make that gingerbread or are you just trying to conjure it up?"

No idea how long I was standing there with my major wax paper revelations. Where else in my life was I sticking with the holed waxed paper when I could move on to something better?

A perfect example is those moments to question "the mandatory"—I just love when it pops up: "Mom, there is a fund-raiser tonight, by the way, at (insert restaurant here), and we have to go. Sorry I forgot to tell you. Starts in fifteen minutes." Yeah, not a need, more of a teaching moment (as I call upon my intention to not run like a last-minute spaz just because that's what "everyone" is doing). "So, they give ten percent back to the group?" I inquire. "Hmm. Our family will spend about seventy-five dollars on the dinner there. We would all have to massively scramble to get there and rearrange the twenty other things going on tonight. So, here is $7.50, no make it an even $10. Give it to the team and we're good." Team makes out, even more so. We don't have to rush there, be late, hurry through a dinner, and miss other commitments. We actually save $65 as well. Just sayin'. Of course, we go to support fund-raisers as our schedules allow,, but I no longer grind myself and my family into the ground to get there because it's "expected". And, with my knowing, I certainly don't owe anyone an explanation. Judgers gonna judge.

My aha was that I had quite a bit of unlearning to do of the illusions that had been built into my life over time from cultural messages, my own insecurities and fear of failure. I committed to replacing these illusions with my true story instead.

"Why shift your illusions? To live the story of your creation."

—Lynn Bodnar

WHAT GRATITUDE REALLY IS AND HOW
I INFUSE IT IN EVERYTHING

I thought I was thankful. I counted my blessings. I helped people in need and saw how thankful I should be: "Thank you that I can shower regularly," kind of thing. I was often told how grateful I should be because I am home with my kids, which I was, but because I was told I *should* feel that way, the gratitude got diluted, y'know?

I'd heard over and over about how being thankful is important to your world, your state, and even impacts what you receive. And like I said, I thought I was thankful. I could spell out a good dozen things—boom, boom, boom— if ever asked.

But, alas, I didn't often fully, deeply, completely FEEL the gratitude.

Instead of gratitude being a list to check off, I discovered it's a place of thinking from, a mind-set, an intentional immersion in gratefulness and something I would have to be aware to be present to. What does that mean? It means proactively thinking of something I was thankful for (or even simply noticing or searching for it). I focused on it: How did it come about? Why am I thankful? Why does this matter? What would it feel like to not have this? I breathed it in and got a smile on my face or maybe even emotional at times, with the big and the little stuff. Even if by all appearances something was unpleasant I could choose to find something to be thankful for, even if it was just having options to brain-storm away the problem.

Sometimes just getting in my Cheerios-infested minivan, starting it up, and going where I need to go gives me great gratitude. It's not a nice new car, but I am so thankful for the memories of ALL that has happened in this van and the fact that it still dutifully takes me from point A to point B.

This kind of gratitude is also self-care because I see and feel all the ways I'm taken care of. I focus on the great stuff and know I will still be supported to manage and navigate the not so great stuff.

Gratitude is another key tool in the toolbox of life satisfaction. Practicing it helps my life to stay on task, more fulfilled and tethered to my purpose. So many times with my family, my active gratitude reminds me what it's all about. What do I want to be grateful for at the end of my life? Great question. I get to answer it daily.

The "comfort food" of gratitude would have been very helpful with the discovery of being pregnant with my bonus baby. I could have had the knowing, the assurance that I would be okay, taken care of, and I could have been so much calmer. Not blown by the wind. Not searching for support and meaning and assurance from other places. I would have known to pause, think, and focus on the good of all the things to be thankful for that the situation made possible. And now, I find myself grateful for the opportunity to have learned all of this through the experience, through the shock, and from the gift.

So gratitude had a cage match with my habitual negativity. Negativity tried hard. It came up with trying to convince me that I had to always know what to do and manage all aspects of the household single-handedly because that was my job.

As in no office hours, no work-life balance, and vacations were the same work in a different location with a ton of extra arrangements. But gratitude dominated by simply pointing out that I get to control my world. Make those decisions with my competency and with my own priorities. My brain became so full with deliberate gratitude looking at situations and obligations through a different lens that no room was left, and the previously negative default had to go.

"There is a reason embracing gratitude is so popular — it changes what you focus on and brings more of it."

— Lynn Bodnar

THE JOURNEY TO THE OTHER SIDE OF
JUDGMENT, VIA VULNERABILITY

As my shocking pregnancy news made the rounds, and the more pelted with comments I was, the more vulnerable I felt. The more uncertain, sad, stuck, lonely, frustrated, emotionally exposed and unheard I became. As I later thought about it, it occurred to me that there are so many criticism-rich situations around moms, momming, and children: I wonder what comments rain down on women and how they feel if they have a lot of kids? If they don't have any children? How about very young moms? Stepmoms? Foster moms? Moms who homeschool? Moms who travel frequently for their job? Single moms? Moms with one leg? Moms with stars upon thars?

Like the story of my friend who was eating dinner out at a family restaurant with her husband and little kids. Kids naturally need training on how this works, and the evening for her was going just okay—some loudness, not bad, definite food globs on the floor. But overall, she felt she was managing it reasonably. As they were finishing their meal, an elderly woman came up and handed her a note. Thinking it may be a warm and fuzzy note saying something like, "enjoy every moment, it goes so fast," she read the note. Instead, the note was one of judgment about how awful and misbehaved her kids were, and shame on her (the mom, not the dad) for bringing them in public for dinner. Unbelievable.

She felt discouraged. Mom shaming alive and well. From another woman who was most likely a mom. Rather than automatically taking on the criticism and hurt, it begs the question—whose issue was this really?

I originally thought I was just oversensitive or just read into the comments that were being made about my chosen profession. I tried to convince myself that it wasn't really as marginalized and stigmatized as it seemed. Then I ran across a TEDx Oxbridge talk by Ben Young. He brought up many interesting points about attitudes toward stay-at-home moms, including, what's with the focus on the hyphenated stay-at-home part? Do we say sit-in-cubicle business analyst? Fly-on-planes management consultant? Stay-at-desk project manager? Even more telling, he once Googled, just to see what the fill-in words that pop up would be for "stay-at-home moms are…" The first four words were: lazy, annoying, pathetic, and the worst. Maybe it wasn't me after all.

Looking at judgment introspectively and overtly, I wondered about its effect on moms as a group. With all this judgment, imposed expectations of perfection, and resulting criticism, it is no wonder we are fragmented as a group, us moms. As I said before, aren't we all aiming for the same thing, trying to raise our kids as best as possible for "success"? Aren't we all eligible for support, grace, love, understanding, validation, and release from perfection?

Feeling vulnerable with a new baby and distancing myself from the "interesting" comments regarding my impossible bonus baby helped me embrace being who and what I am. I realized, the only shame really was what others created in their thinking and crazy comments. It was on them, but it still hurt, and it hurts us all because the price paid is a lack of togetherness and support when we most need each other.

I can't help but notice that we could all appreciate our similarities and differences more as we each live out our stories. We are all in it together, and we all want the best for our kids. We moms need each other. We understand the similar job we are all walking through, the hopes we all have raising our children with no guarantees. So what if we get there differently? Why judge each other? Why cut down or try to be superior? Why create a gulf with assumptions? It doesn't elevate anyone, it only degrades everyone. We don't understand what someone is going through or why they do what they do, so why not try to assume the best? Or send a little love and encouragement their way in your thoughts or simply by holding the door open for them? You don't have to make a batch of cookies or take their kids for a weekend— often a kind smile could be all someone needs.

I was earnestly seeking real, true change and growth— my serious face and big-girl underpants. I had been jolted, via my unexpected bundle of joy, causing me to look fully at what this role of mom has become. Why was I so worried about not screwing up my kids' lives irreparably, the drive to seem "together" and be Facebook ready at all times? Why did it seem moms felt they had to "do it all"? Living this way, and hiding behind a mask, is exhausting. So, when moms are exhausted, it's not only from lack of sleep. It's from trying to do it all and to maintain the illusion of handling it all perfectly.

It's a process of uncertainty, risk and emotional exposure (the definition of vulnerability by Brene Brown). It can be trying and lonely, just like momming. Some may see it as only ugly, but becoming real to yourself includes emerging through the judgment and embracing the vulnerability. Even if others do not get you, some always will, even if it's just you.

I LOVE the way the Velveteen Rabbit sorts it out:

He said, "*You become. It takes a long time. That's why it doesn't happen often to people who break easily or have sharp edges, or who have to be carefully kept. Generally, by the time you are Real, most of your hair has been loved off, and your eyes drop out and you get loose in the joints and very shabby. But these things don't matter at all, because once you are Real you can't be ugly except to people who don't understand.*"

The beautiful a-ha for me was the power in vulnerably owning who I really was and finding that it wasn't weakness but delicious courage. Opening up allowed me to see judgment of each other for what it is—separating moms who need each other, eroding empathy, and, in reality, mostly damaging the one who judges. I was ready to change that. So, I changed me.

"Vulnerability sounds like truth and feels like courage. Truth and courage aren't always comfortable but they are never weakness."

— Brené Brown

THE JOY-INDUCING QUEST OF "LIGHTENING UP" & HUMOR PROCUREMENT

"If you can laugh at this later, you can laugh at this now," became part of my mantra. Humor is always welcome in my world, even during the hard times. Maybe especially during the hard times. I determined to find the humor in things and do a lot more laughing. After all, this child rearing thing is a journey, not a race. And it can be hilarious. It was time to lighten up and drink in the humor brought to me each day.

Being able to lighten up, you guessed it, took time. There were generationally ingrained habits and expectations to live up to (and examine closely) after all. I started simply. Like, I noticed that birth to the bonus baby had in fact taken place, after all the denial, so, quite literally I had already lightened up some.

We moms live a hypervigilant life. We have to be on top of so much simultaneously, and yes, it's life or death. Think electrocution, poisoning, broken bones, choking, house escape, and so much more. Like things that you didn't even think of as being possible. I didn't know a little person could actually have both ends activated at the same time, let alone three kids at once… huh. At least that's not a 911 call. But I did call my mom to be able to laugh about it between bucket cleanups.

They say moms have eyeballs in the back of our heads for a reason. And for the record it's true. When you become a mom, you grow a pair—capable of seeing all—and the superpowers to multi-manage and mega-task. So, have some fun with your superpowers. Mess with your kids and keep them wondering. Summon your sense of humor as often as possible. Make others laugh. Search out things that are funny. Collect your favorite memes or funny pictures and have them scroll ready on your phone.

Then, there is joy listing. It's the cool and hip friend of self-care. The idea is to identify 15 or more things that bring you joy that do not cost money and 15 or more things that bring you joy that do cost money. So, I did that. There is something about identifying a thing that brings you joy: when you can do it, experience it, plan it, create it, or it just happens, the joy seems far more magnified and lasting, like my joy when my family is all belly-laughing about something ridiculously funny that bystanders would do the "they are crazy" finger swirl to. Other examples: getting a massage; watching the changing sunset over the mountains, especially with my family (yes, they humor me often); a really good salad with all the goodies I love, made by someone else; little kids' faces at a parade; connecting deeply with a friend; meditating; people greeting arriving passengers at the airport, especially returning military. My list goes on and gets added to all the time.

My epiphany was that by simply making a joy list, it defines the joy, and it just seems to show up more often. Or maybe I showed up for it?

Lastly, the humor procurement part for me also means making the more fun choice, for example: picking the movie that's funny and uplifting over the scary or depressing one, asking people what their favorite joke is (I've got to start writing these down!), observing people and really how cute and fun they are, and just listening to my children and husband, the ultimate comedians on the planet.

"Sometimes your joy is the source of your smile, but sometimes your smile can be the source of your joy."

— Thich Nhat Hanh

CORE LEVEL WELL-BEING

Core level well being really puts it all together, my a-ha's to awakening and it is a function of daily choice. Often moment by moment, even. Not to bounce around like a pinball, but stay in my questioning. What serves my mind, body and soul? What feels good and right for me and others around me? What are my needs of this day — to thrive, fulfill my purpose and experience all the mindful joy possible? Including what tools (like gratitude listing) do I need to call upon to make the very most of this day that I have been given. I get to live this day, expanding and creating what comes next.

Some days my highest level of core well-being could be serving everybody else. That could feel the best to me. It could be showing up for a friend and letting everything else go for that day. It could be licking my wounds or deciding this is the day I move on, forgive. It could be allowing some needed rest and not going to one of my kid's games (what, that's allowed?!). It is a daily vigilance on keeping out the previous regular barrage of negativity and harsh self-criticism that I used to heap on myself, which would even make Eeyore proud. It's the feeling of being in yourself, having your own back, living in possibility and choice.

Life has its difficulties, curveballs, sorrows and agonizing challenges at times. To expect a life to be always smooth sailing is to set yourself up for more pain than necessary. Knowing and realizing beforehand that I'll have to face some tough things, I have come to this conclusion. As best as possible (meaning not perfect), I try to flow, let go, manage what's right in front of me and try not to jump into the whirlpool of the fear-based and infinite, "what if's." Instead I try to look at the other side of the looming disastrous "what if's" and ask the opposite. If all the bad scenarios are possible, why not list all the good ones that are possible? Both sides have a certain infinite probability, right? With the belief and faith that it will be what it will be and that I can trust myself and the support I have to navigate life, all I need to do is show up and do the best I know how along the way. Choose not to give up. I get to learn and live as I go, and even expect the times of fear, difficulty and pain. Not focusing on them or living in "oh no, what's next," but transcending the stifling fear by the beauty of my knowing, the beauty of my decision ahead of time that I will show up and be me. That it is and will be enough.

My core well being is nurtured and nourished through daily decisions, my supportive tools, stillness and acceptance that I am enough, even when I'm not.

"I must try to be alone for part of each year... and part of each day... in order to keep my core, my center...Women must be still as the axis of a wheel in the midst of her activities. She must be the pioneer of achieving this stillness, not only for her own salvation, but for the salvation of family life, of society, perhaps even of our civilization".

—Anne Morrow Lindbergh

I am so grateful for these head-smackin', smile-creating, me-bettering a-ha's in my journey, what I have learned, and how I reframed a new way of life. Sometimes I think, what if I'd never had my bonus baby? What if that shock and massively denied curveball in my plans had never come along? Would I have just zombied along, unaware, spinning my wheels, living in "should-ville"? Thankfully, I'll never know. I wouldn't wish away this life-changing experience, my beautiful daughter and expanded family, for anything.

The New Story

How did a bonus baby, later in life and being unknowingly "stuck" in my narrowly defined role of mom, actually deliver a new me? Because I chose to watch the movie of mothering over again. And catch so much more. Prompting the decision to not sleepwalk through life doing the "should's", hoping to measure up and fit in, but questioning what I was creating every day, for myself and others. I had control of my own thoughts, my personal reality, and new tools were available to support me in the wonderful journey of motherhood.

Starting over with another child, some would say a "curveball", gave me the revelation:

Being a mom doesn't define me but instead it refines me.

I found my value, wholeness, and purpose with intentionality and joy.

As I've delved into my learnings, my a-ha's, with new experiences and exposure to new people and ideas, I've found a happier me with a healthier mindset, while scraping off the sticky and insidious idea of perfectionism. Key ingredients of this mix required being gentle and accepting of myself. I also became abundantly clear that I desired to be uber mindful— because it is so important—of what I say to others and how I say it. Recognizing that I am fully worthy and enough, as is, and so is everyone else. Mind you, it's an ongoing project, especially for this late bloomer. My tombstone could very well include, "Dang, she just got started."

Your story is unique. You live and create it daily. Yes, YOU create it. You define who you are and decide what you focus on from the moment you wake and those thoughts start to churn, to how the day unfolds with your perspective and choices guiding you, until you place your head back on that pillow at night. You get to be you. You don't need permission. And you certainly don't need to *try* to be perfect—because you already are.

It's your story—your daily "momoir". Own it. Own you. Write it with awareness, love, gratitude, and self-trust. Because of the fact that you are breathing and on this planet, you already are worthy. And you really already are perfect, Cupcake.

Recipe

HOW TO MAKE A "REAL" MOM

1 part Openness:
use the true and pure, honest brand

1 part Awareness:
not the generic default, use quality from scratch

1 part Beliefs:
separated, keeping the fresh ones

1 part (Shifted) Illusions:
best used with high quality awareness

1 part Intentionality:
all the flavors of your choosing

1 part Self-Care:
of very high quality, consistently stirred in

1 part Judgment Reduction:
with Vulnerability enhancements

1 part Heart-Centeredness:
add to middle of mix, allow it to expand out and then blend in thoroughly

1 part Lighten Up:
fluff up entire mix with humor and belly laughs. You'll find this ingredient everywhere, just look

Instructions

Combine all the ingredients,
pour them into your life, and let them rise up to make you
fully, joyously and spectacularly YOU!

WRITE YOUR MOMOIR

Look for the companion guide to "The Perfect Cupcake". A self-guided journey to awakening, aligning and illusion shifting through your art of momliness to a joyously intentional life (without having to have another baby).

Lynn Bodnar
the heart of the matter

ABOUT THE AUTHOR

Lynn Bodnar's greatest personal discovery was that motherhood didn't actually define her, but instead refined her. With that awakening, she became a mom-advocate and passionate about asking better questions about motherhood (especially inside her own head). Lynn's diverse experiences include being an Amazon best selling author, an anti-human trafficking campaigner for a non-profit, a volunteer sign language interpreter, a relocation specialist in Germany, a lifeguard (which actually came in handy), a recipe-ologist, and the original Uber driver (for select clientele and never once tipped).

Grateful to be living an intentional life—traveling, learning, laughing, growing, and supporting women to shift their illusions—Lynn encourages moms everywhere to write their own story, with awareness, every day. If you feel the vibe of this kind of mom-village and want to join the conversation, get in touch. You already belong.

Lynn lives in Colorado with her husband, four children, one dog, and incredible gratitude.

WWW.LYNNBODNAR.COM

GRATITUDES

I've received so much encouragement on many levels to pursue this book. Many times, the right person was there to remind me I could do this when I was nervous or doubtful.

Thank you to my family, and you know who you are... even though you thought this was about you, this story really is about me (being focused on you).

To my parents for loving me, always doing their best, and letting that sixteen-year-old boy with the crazy hair hang around.

To those who have been emotionally invested, way beyond encouraging, reading stuff, giving feedback (over and over), listening to my ramblings (and still answered the phone again), refusing to get bored, giving generously of your intellect and time and are at the heart of what village and friendship and love are: Leslie Judd, Donna Cuddemi, Julie Margo, Cyndee Jardieu and Chelsea Jewell.

To the incredible support I am blessed and surrounded with: Sarah Zeren, Scott and Kelley Brink, Susan Fitch, Jessica Mullen, Hayley Bammesberger, Emily Bernatow, Sara Sanders, Jannie Williams, Julie Larkin, Jodie Howard, Madeleine Eno, Diane Fromme, Madeleine Faiella, Jeanette Lundell, Tara Tooley, Michelle McCollough, Whitney and Kevin Williams, and Robert and Kara Helms.

To the wise counsel and beautiful designs Chelsea Jewell creates.

To the creative ideas and the fun getting there from Dayton Williams.

To the sisterhood of the Inner Circle. Always connected, always cheering for each other.

To Kyle Wilson and Takara Sights, for their original nudging and ongoing support.

Thank you, life-changers: Brené Brown, Chad Hymas, Mother Mary, Tiffany Peterson, Anne Morrow Lindberg, Dorothy Bodnar, Fran Bodnar Ores and so many others.

Thank you to mothers everywhere, working it day in and day out—you've got this, you inspire me. Thanks for showing up. Thanks for being at the heart of the matter.

Made in the USA
Columbia, SC
26 November 2019